THE FLETCHER SCHOOL OF LAW AND DIPLOMACY
A Graduate School of International Affairs
Administered with the Cooperation of Harvard University
TUFTS UNIVERSITY · MEDFORD, MASSACHUSETTS

DIPLOMACY
IN THE
NUCLEAR AGE

THE WILLIAM L. CLAYTON LECTURES
ON INTERNATIONAL ECONOMIC
AFFAIRS AND FOREIGN POLICY · 1958

LESTER B. PEARSON

DIPLOMACY
IN THE
NUCLEAR
AGE

1959
HARVARD UNIVERSITY PRESS
CAMBRIDGE, MASSACHUSETTS

Library of Congress Catalog Card Number 59–11514
Printed in the United States of America
Published in Great Britain by Oxford University Press, London
Published in Canada by S. J. Reginald Saunders and Company, Limited

THE WILLIAM L. CLAYTON LECTURES

The William L. Clayton Center for International Economic Affairs was established in 1952 at the Fletcher School of Law and Diplomacy, Tufts University, in honor and recognition of Mr. Clayton's services as one of the country's leading business-statesmen and its first Under Secretary of State for Economic Affairs. Mr. Clayton is founder and retired head of Anderson, Clayton & Company, the world's largest cotton merchants. His public service includes the following offices: Assistant Secretary of Commerce, 1942–44; Administrator of the Surplus War Property Administration; Assistant Secretary of State, 1944–46; and Under Secretary of State for Economic Affairs, 1946–48.

The foundation of the William L. Clayton Center was officially sponsored by the American Cotton Shippers Association, honoring "the accomplishments of Mr. Clayton both in the international cotton trade and as a public servant in the field of economic diplomacy," and "as a means of recognizing his substantial service to the Nation and extending the influence of his example in the field of international trade and diplomacy." Some two hundred individuals, business firms, banks and foundations — principally connected with the cotton trade — joined in contributing the endowment for the Clayton Center.

The program of the Clayton Center — devoted to education and research — includes the William L. Clayton Professorship of International Economic Affairs, a program of research and current policy studies, a program of Clayton Fellowships to encourage and assist outstanding young men and women to prepare for careers in international economic affairs and diplomacy, and the annual Clayton Lectures by persons distinguished in the field of diplomacy, trade or scholarship in international affairs. The Clayton Lectures were inaugurated by former Secretary of State Dean Acheson, in October 1957, on the subject, "Power and Diplomacy." The 1958 Clayton Lectures by the Honorable Lester Bowles Pearson marked the Twenty-Fifth Anniversary of the founding of the Fletcher School of Law and Diplomacy, October 27, 1933.

The text of the address given by Mr. Pearson upon receiving the award of the Nobel Peace Prize for 1957 is also included in this volume, with the kind permission of the Clayton Lecture Committee.

CONTENTS

DIPLOMACY
IN THE
NUCLEAR AGE

I DIPLOMACY NEW AND OLD: TECHNIQUES AND FUNCTIONS

I consider it a great honor and no small responsibility to give the William L. Clayton Lectures for 1958. The man after whom they are named, and who made them possible, has served his country well and wisely for many years, and I will always consider it a privilege to have worked with him in the quest for better relations between peoples.

No one could have been more honest and forthright than Will Clayton in presenting the American viewpoint on the international questions with which he had to deal. But his sturdy and frank Americanism never prevented him from doing everything he could to bring about that reconciliation of the requirements of nationalism and internationalism which is essential if we are ever to achieve security and prosperity in a peaceful world.

The subject of these Lectures, "Diplomacy in the Nuclear Age," has, perhaps, more relevancy to power than to diplomacy. The release of atomic energy which initiated the nuclear age has, of course, profoundly affected the making of foreign policy, by introducing among other things new and far-reaching concepts of defense and strategy. It has not affected the conduct of diplomacy as such, though it has made the consequences of failure far more disastrous than formerly, if that failure should lead to war.

In the past, diplomatic setbacks have not necessarily been fatal, or always even serious. This was in large part due to the differentiation that was clearly established between the formation of policy and its execution. Only the latter is diplomacy in the strict and classical meaning of the word. Diplomacy does not make policy, it transmits and explains it and tries to negotiate arrangements which embody and secure it.

There is, however, a growing tendency now to confuse the two, policy and diplomacy, by combining their functions. Policy makers are increasingly becoming their own diplomatic agents. The consequences of diplomatic failure can therefore be serious indeed, far more serious than formerly. They can more easily and more directly lead to wars which in the nuclear age could mean, literally, extinction.

The conduct of diplomacy, however, as contrasted with its results, has not been affected by the nuclear age as much as it has by two developments that I would like to mention: first, the amazing acceleration of communications, and, second, the transformation of political society in so many parts of the world.

Recent sweeping and sensational advances in the science and technology of communications have brought about such far-reaching changes in the practice of diplomacy as to affect even its principles. They have drastically altered the tempo and hence the temper of diplomacy. In an easier, slower-moving age tensions were often less, or at least seemed less, because the tempo was slower. Movement does not always mean progress. Speed at times generates only friction. Nor does it always get the oiling and greasing against such friction which are required. This may help to explain some of the results of the triphammer techniques used occasionally now in so-called diplomacy.

Modern communications have also brought peoples and nations very close together. Propinquity does not, of course, invariably make for peace, as even the most happily domesticated husband and wife will testify. Closer, if not easier, contacts and the conquest of distance do have a bearing, however, on diplomacy. They have brought about significant changes in modern diplomatic practice.

Such changes, in fact, became inevitable once an ambassador became a person at the receiving end of a cable or wireless communication. His relative independence then disappeared, along with much of his power to influence policy as well as to channel it as he saw fit to the government to which he was accredited. It also left him with new problems of time and space. It is difficult enough to receive, to act on, and report on instructions all within a few hours. It is even worse to read in the press about those instructions before they are received, as well as about the action you have taken or not taken regarding them within an hour or so after you have made your report.

The other development which I have mentioned — and it is of equal or greater importance in its effect on diplomatic method — is the transformation of political society in the last century. Among more than a third of the people of the world, this transformation has led from old-fashioned autocracy of one kind or another to Communist dictatorship. Yet the diplomacy practiced by a representative of these states is not in essence different from that of the delegate of any earlier despotism. He has little or no freedom of action or maneuver, and if he loses his case, he may even lose his head.

The manners and methods of the Communist diplomat, however, have reflected the proletarian nature of the revolution in his country. They are characterized by toughness, a brutal use of words, an obstinate refusal to admit of two sides to any argument, and an attitude of suspicious restraint, though this is changing, in social-official contacts.

There is also an inflexibility about his tactics which probably stems from the centralization of all policy in a small group, or in one man, in Moscow. Woe betide the Communist representative who departs one iota from the instructions, or perhaps even the argument, sent him from headquarters — unless, of course, he happens, and this is very rare, to be headquarters himself. At United Nations assemblies, it is often not possible to get a comma changed in a single resolution which a Communist delegation has accepted without a reference back to somebody or something at home.

The other transformation of political society, which we call democratization, has meant something quite different for diplomacy. Because of it, democratic foreign policy and diplomatic negotiation now have to conform to the day-by-day desires and dictates of an electorate, that is, to mass public opinion. Today everyone who reads a newspaper headline or the news of the week in capsule form becomes an expert in foreign policy and diplomacy. Neither is, fortunately or unfortunately, an exact science like nuclear physics or bridge building or chess.

Sir Harold Nicolson, who has written with wit and wisdom about diplomacy, has put it this way: "The art of diplomacy, as that of water colours, has suffered much from the fascination which it exercises on the amateur." Lord Strang, formerly permanent Under-Secretary in the British Foreign Office, expressed the same feeling more seriously when he said: "In a world where war is everybody's tragedy and everybody's nightmare, diplomacy is everybody's business."

Foreign policy and diplomacy are today, therefore, subject to the control and to the vagaries of a public opinion which is now the target of a ceaseless and organized battering by all the media of mass communication which enlighten and confuse us. True, public opinion may at times be merely the self-interest of a pressure group or the prejudiced viewpoint of a vocal minority which a timid government mistakes for the true voice of the people. However that may be, the effect on diplomacy has been the same. It has become more exposed to public pressures and public tastes. It has also lost its exclusive and aristocratic tradition. Envoys are now, more and more, becoming either hardworking professional civil servants trying to live on their salaries, or rich political nominees very suspicious, or pretending to be so, of gold braid and striped pants.

More important, though, than these changes themselves, is the effect they have had on that development which I have already mentioned, the mixing of policy and diplomacy. This mixing became unavoidable, I suppose, once a foreign minister could fly to another capital thousands of miles away for face-to-face discussions with his opposite number, and in less time than a resident ambassador thought it proper to take in the last century when he was instructed to call on the foreign minister.

With easy communications for bilateral talks, with

all the useful publicity that might result, with international conferences for multilateral talks, quickly assembled and spectacularly publicized, policy makers are now tempted to conduct their own diplomacy. So policy and diplomacy increasingly become intermingled, often to the benefit of neither.

This process of substituting diplomacy by ministerial conference for diplomacy through envoys, brought about by both technical and political developments, was accelerated by World War I. The impression was then created, and became both popular and widespread, that somehow this tragedy was the result of secret professional diplomacy.

Gordon Craig, in an article in *World Politics* of January 1952 on "The Professional Diplomat and His Problems," quotes a member of the British House of Commons as saying in March 1918: "The old Ambassadorial system has failed and is discredited in the eyes of most people. After the war, the old diplomacy of Court and upper classes will be in the eyes of most people, obsolete and inadequate."

This was the prevailing opinion, and politicians responded to it with alacrity and approval. Hence there began the era of ministerial diplomacy by conference, the most enthusiastic practitioner of which at that time was Mr. Lloyd George, who believed that diplomats were invented to wear knee-breeches and to waste time, and should not be permitted to speak for democracies. This should be left, he thought, to elected representatives of the people.

Political diplomacy can, of course, in some circumstances be useful, even essential. It does bring the makers of policy face to face and gives them the opportunity to get to know each other. Good results no doubt can flow from that knowledge. Friendship, as well as enmity, can result from personal contact.

The road to understanding can at times be made easier; road-blocks to such understanding can be cleared or at least exposed when policy makers get together either on summits, where winds blow hard and the footing is often precarious, or more comfortably in valleys, where the climate can be calmer and the surroundings more relaxing.

Personal and political diplomacy, however, has also important disadvantages, and even dangers. If governments fail to reach agreement through official diplomatic channels, they can go on trying or, at worst, fail without fury. Political face can be saved by allowing diplomatic heads to fall. But when foreign ministers or, even more, when chiefs of governments meet, with their retinue of press, radio, and television companions, with experts, advisers, and advisers to advisers, things become more complicated and often more difficult.

There is also the danger that, if agreement cannot be reached at meetings on which so much public hope and expectation have been centered, this will be interpreted as conclusive evidence that agreement never will be possible. The reaction to this may be, in its turn, unnecessarily pessimistic, with unhappy political results. Consequently, there is always a strong temptation to conceal or deny the fact of failure or to concentrate on blaming the other person or persons for it.

In the latter technique the Communists are past masters. Their participation at international conferences is, in fact, often for propaganda purposes only. Their tactics to this end are worked out long before a conference opens, and their exploitation of failure by attributing it to others continues long after the conference ends.

Whatever the disadvantages may be, quick and easy communications, the pressures of public opinion, and the proclaimed values of personal contact (prize fighters also have very close personal contact) have made personal diplomacy by policy makers quite common. As Lord Strang has put it: "It is small wonder that in the climate of today a Minister may sometimes be tempted to jump into an aircraft with only a general idea of his policy, with no precisely defined formulation of it, and go and talk around a table with his opposite number in the hope that, by a kind of joint improvisation, something useful may come out of the meeting. The temptation is to think that a conference is a substitute for a policy."

It was not always so. In other days the prime ministers and foreign ministers — except in times of great emergency and usually even then — stayed home. Perhaps it was merely because traveling difficulties made distance seem so great and journeys so time-consuming; or perhaps they acted on the principle praised by Philippe de Comines some centuries back when he said: "Two great princes who wish to establish good personal relations should never meet each other face-to-face but ought to communicate through good and wise ambassadors."

Before the twentieth century, then, ministers devoted their time and energy to working out policies on the advice of their experts — with some thought, of course, for Parliament or Congress, or Assembly, but little for the "people" and none at all for Gallup polls. Ambassadors executed these policies, with considerable pomp and circumstance, and by their manner of doing so, as I have said, often influenced them.

The whole glamorous business of those days is far removed from 1959 when the policy makers take a decisive and direct part in the processes of diplomatic negotiation, either at great international congresses or by flying visits to their opposite number. Moreover, all such activity is conducted under the white light of the most intense publicity, with the details of all discussions and negotiations appearing in the five o'clock editions and their meaning clarified and interpreted by television and radio commentators an hour or so later.

These publicity pressures can — as I shall try to show later — prejudice, and sometimes even prevent good results from diplomatic negotiation. They have also had an important effect on diplomatic procedures, and on the position of the diplomat. His role, in fact, now often includes responsibility for the problems and the opportunities of publicity which arise out of ministerial diplomacy.

While the policy makers argue and orate, the ambassador, sitting alongside or behind his political chief, may have to keep the press and radio informed of what is going on and insure that the public relations are working smoothly. Then, before the next day's proceedings, the news dispatches have to be carefully scanned to find out what was reported as being said, especially at the secret meetings. In diplomacy in the age of popular democracy there is nothing true or false until you find out what some person, who writes or comments and who has the audience of one million or ten million, has said about it.

This press and public relations function can be, in truth, a very important part of the diplomat's activity. But here also the ambassador is often short-circuited. The press officer who accompanies his foreign minister, and is usually very close to him, may make the pronouncements and give the interpretations when the meeting is over. This official has now become a most important cog in the diplomatic machine. His importance is a tribute to the influence of opinion on policy and to the necessity of selling your product to millions of consumers, the electorate.

The man responsible for this salesmanship operation is often a harassed and hard-pressed ex-reporter, working in front of cameras, microphones, and a hundred wolves who call him "Joe" and who cajole or bully him into intimate disclosures about the most personal as well as the most political matters. He has to be a skillful practitioner of what might be called press "brinkmanship." Yet his activity is certainly diplomatic in accordance with a modern meaning of the word.

In one way or another, however, public relations, if not press relations, have always been a main preoccupation of the good diplomat. A hundred years ago it was an aristocrat from Virginia or a belted earl who was trying to influence a monarch or another aristocrat. It was done with great decorum — though often with polished and courteous deceit — and nobody read anything about it next morning or even next year. Today it means the task of cultivating, not only the head of a government or a cabinet minister, but the press, trade unions, opposition political chiefs, television and radio commentators, and the League of Women Voters.

A successful practitioner of the "new diplomacy"

must be a very versatile person, doing more things than were ever required or would have been thought seemly, in the past. Lord Stratford de Redcliffe, or Talleyrand, or John Quincy Adams would have been shocked and horrified if he had been asked, as part of his duty, to kick off at a football game or address a service club at luncheon and be called "John." Lord Lyons was five years British Ambassador in Washington in the latter half of the nineteenth century without ever having made a speech or, perhaps what is even more startling, ever having taken a drink. These things are now a part, and often a very important part, of a diplomat's work. They can even be agreeable.

Yet, as I have just said, though the procedures and methods have drastically changed, the good diplomat has, in one way or another, always been a propagandist — or, if you like the expression better, a disseminator of views and opinions. Many centuries ago, as recounted by Sardar Panikkar, the distinguished Indian diplomat, Sri Krishna, a Hindu special emissary to a foreign court, described his mission as follows: "I shall go to the Kaurava court to present your case in the best light, to try and get them to accept your demands; and if my efforts fail and war becomes inevitable we shall show the world how we are right and they are wrong so that the world may not misjudge between us." In other words, his mission was not only one for negotiation but also a propaganda and public relations one. So, in essence, it always has been in diplomacy from Sri Krishna to Demosthenes to Cardinal Richelieu to the press counselor and cultural attaché of any embassy in 1959.

In these days, however, the means and mechanics of propaganda and public relations are much more efficient than they used to be and the audience is much greater. It is everybody.

An offshoot of this propaganda function of diplomacy is the emphasis now laid on spreading the best of your culture in other countries, on creating a cultivated soil in which the flowers of good will, political favor, and economic advantage can grow. For this purpose you must reach the masses. This can be done in any free society by appealing directly to them, though it has to be done with discretion. It is not possible even to attempt it behind the iron curtain, something which may seem to put our diplomacy at a considerable disadvantage.

Sardar Panikkar has this to say about cultural propaganda and diplomatic mass appeal, which has been exploited so skillfully by Communist governments for their own purposes, and from which they themselves have blocked foreign governments: "By deliberately directing propaganda to other countries and appealing to the proletariat, the communists have widened the scope of international relations. In the days of old diplomacy international relations were between Governments. In New Diplomacy an attempt is being made to establish such relations directly with the people. A part of the machinery of this new international relations consists of organizations like the various 'new democratic' bodies, e.g., the Democratic Women's Association, the Peace Front, the progressive literature societies, People's Theatre, etc. This kind of activity is not confined to the Soviet camp. The Voice of America attempts to reach the masses directly in Russia, China and other countries and convert them to the American way of life." It should be pointed out here that the attempt can only be made against great obstacles and cannot in present circumstances be very effective.

Sardar Panikkar goes on: " 'Cultural' organizations preach the greatness of Free Enterprise. How far this kind of diplomacy has become a permanent feature of international life may be judged by the fact that a Press Attaché and an information section are now considered essential to an Ambassador's establishment. In some Embassies there are officers enjoying the strange title of Cultural Attaché. This attempt to sell culture to other countries is perhaps a reflex action to the ideological propaganda indulged in by some countries. But so far as I know this aspect of international relations, though it has added greatly to expenditure of Embassies, has not contributed anything substantial to a better understanding between nations."

Where have these developments, these new functions, applied in a new way, where have they left the trained and experienced professional? Is he now primarily a 'front-man' to give cocktail parties, to meet planes, or entertain congressmen who are increasingly getting into the diplomatic game themselves, traveling and representing and intervening and explaining?

Not at all. He still has important and responsible work to do, as I know from the experience of having been one and, later, as a Foreign Minister, from having greatly benefited by their skilled and loyal services. I wish only that more advantage were taken of their training and experience.

Certainly the observing and reportorial functions of the professional diplomat remain. The ability and knowledge to sense what is going on and to inform and warn his own government is still important, as is the supplying of political intelligence as a basis for the policy at home toward the state to which he is accredited. Even here, however, there are rivals in the foreign correspondents of newspapers whose dispatches can be as full, shrewd, and useful as any diplomat's. Sometimes they are based on an even greater knowledge and broader experience of the country — and its people — about which they are both writing.

The professional diplomat retains other and even more responsible functions. He may find himself during a sudden crisis in the very center of diplomatic negotiations, operating at times on ambiguous instructions or on no instructions at all. The ease of communications that I have mentioned doesn't always mean speed in deciding at home what or how to communicate. So the diplomatic representative, even today, may at times have to make important decisions on his own responsibility and hope that his government will back him up. Sometimes he may be deliberately left out on a limb five thousand miles from home, while argument goes on within his own government as to what to do about it.

When his position is a happier and a more normal one and he has his instructions, he can still cause a great deal of harm if he carries out those instructions ineptly, just as he can be of the greatest assistance to his government when he carries them out skillfully.

He can also serve his country well by making friends for it in the country to which he is accredited, and by explaining the policies of his government in such a way as to put them in the best possible light. Today this requires, as we have seen, that he should reach and impress a far wider audience than a monarch and his court.

Indeed his audience may even include groups or elements in opposition to the government in power. He will need to show a maximum of diplomacy here. He will have to be far more careful than were the diplomats a few centuries ago who interfered quite openly in domestic affairs, more openly than even the most fanatic Communist envoy would dare today. Indeed, a diplomatic duke of the sixteenth or seventeenth century often became as "subversive," and was expelled with as much contumely, as any Communist diplomat today in a Fascist dictatorship or any Western diplomat in a Communist country. In the 16th, 17th, and even 18th centuries, diplomats considered it part of their normal duty, in protecting and advancing the interests of their state, to foment internal opposition to the government of the country to which they were accredited if that government seemed unfriendly. Indeed, on this score so great was the suspicion of foreign ambassadors in England in the 17th century, that in 1653 a law was passed there to the effect that any member of Parliament who spoke to one was to be deprived of his seat in the House of Commons. It is not surprising, then, that in those times the movements and the contacts of diplomats were as supervised and restricted as they are in Communist Russia or China today.

It was only after the Congress of Vienna in 1815 that the profession became internationally privileged and honored. From that year until World War I there was a period of classic and, on the whole, constructive diplomacy, practiced for the most part by professionals whose manners — if not always their objectives — were in strong contrast with those often in evidence today.

Something else, however, than bad manners has been added to the "new diplomacy." The envoys today, in our complex international society, include many who are neither "professionals" nor "politicians," many who technically have no diplomatic credentials at all and whose activities would not have been recognized a few decades ago as having any official significance. Yet now their influence on the prestige and the position of their country abroad can be great.

They are a new international species, moving around the world serving their corporations and their governments, and also, through the United Nations or other international agencies, their fellowmen. They are experts in many phases of social, economic, or scientific activity, and they can be important in the new type of diplomacy. A soil scientist from the United States in Afghanistan may, while he is there, do more to influence Afghan opinion on United States policy, for better or for worse, than the United States or even the Soviet ambassador.

An ambassador in Ryadh or in Teheran may have as many dealings with Trans-Desert Petroleum, Inc., as he has with his own foreign office. Indeed, there may be times when he may wonder which is which.

It is a function of today's diplomacy, at headquarters and in the field, to coordinate and if possible to control in the national interest many of these disparate and at times even conflicting activities. It certainly helps to make career diplomacy a "sweat-shirt" rather than a "boiled-shirt" kind of work.

Yet, in spite of everything, the old tradition of glamor and privilege and exclusiveness somehow persists. I wonder why. Perhaps it is a hangover from the "Colonel of The Red Hussars" type of fiction or from the appearance of paperback editions of the Memoirs of Count X or Duc de Y at the Congresses of Berlin or Vienna in the good old days. Or perhaps it is kept alive by advertisements which show the Envoy Extraordinary, with a broad red ribbon over his stiff white shirt, sipping a rare old brandy, while his aristocratic face above his well-trimmed imperial shows well-bred appreciation.

All that, of course, has gone, but the melody and the memory linger on, fortified by such things as diplomatic privilege, which permits a Third Secretary to park in front of a hydrant without a fine, and to buy duty-free beverages so that he may give cocktail parties and worm secrets out of the beautiful spies of fiction, who, unfortunately, are now usually middle-aged stenographers in the Bureau of the Budget or harassed clerks in the Agency for Coordinating Travel in Outer Space.

Times and manners change but the qualities of the good diplomat do not alter. What they are should be clear from the nature of the work. They must include those required for a good civil servant and those additional and special ones necessary for a person to represent his country acceptably abroad. They are qualities of both heart and mind. Success in politics, in business, or in a profession does not insure their possession.

Diplomacy, indeed, is itself a profession, and he who would succeed at it needs training and experience as well as aptitude. It is essential, for instance, that a good diplomat should have a knowledge and understanding of the people among whom he is to live and work, of their culture, and traditions and language, their problems, their hopes, their prejudices, and their fears. Democracies in their foreign representation often ignore these requirements and suffer for it; or they subordinate them to considerations which have nothing to do with diplomacy. Communist governments do not often make this mistake, especially in their representation in ex-colonial countries.

A diplomat, it is obvious, must have a persuasive and engaging personality. He must be able to meet people easily and sympathetically and widely. If he confines his social activities to the circle of his official contacts, plus a few of the socially and financially privileged, he will seriously prejudice his usefulness. It is easy for a busy and conscientious diplomat to be quite unaware of what is going on in a country by ignoring those who may be the really important sources of social, economic, and political developments, in favor of the chosen few who may seem to have more to offer him socially and officially. Of course, he can't ignore these — that would be stupid — and he may have to subject himself almost daily to the boring and crushing demands of the large and frothy cocktail party. Sometimes a man in a corner at one of these parties, either in alcohol or in desperation, will give away some interesting and even important information. But if the diplomat never leaves this circle of activity, he will lose much, both personally and officially.

Technical and professional qualifications, however, are not enough. If a diplomat's work, especially his reporting, is to be of value to his government, it must above all be characterized by objectivity and integrity. He must never be influenced by fear or favor. Once an envoy begins to tell the foreign office merely things that he thinks will fit into its ideas of sound policy, or things that could not possibly embarrass him ten years later, then he might as well be a totalitarian envoy, reporting only that which confirms the all-wise and all-powerful leader's views, or Communist theory as interpreted by that leader.

Sir Harold Nicolson has rightly stated that the most important asset for a diplomat is a reputation for honesty and reliability — the qualities that win the respect of others and help him keep his own, that secure for their possessor a reputation as a person on whom, and on whose word, one can count, whose integrity cannot be shaken by the fear of sticks or the hope of carrots.

No diplomat, either of the professional or political variety, can acquire this quality if, in his reports and in his advice, he compromises with his own considered and honest judgment, or if he is too concerned about how that judgment will stand up later before a Congressional or Parliamentary committee.

Sir Harold Nicolson has also written that the mental and moral equipment of a good diplomat in the 15th and 16th centuries was expected to include at least nine ingredients, as follows: "He must realize that all foreigners are regarded with suspicion and must therefore conceal his astuteness and appear as a pleasant man of the world. He must be hospitable and employ an excellent cook. He must be a man of taste and erudition and cultivate the society of writers, artists and scientists. He must be a naturally patient man, willing to spin out negotiations and to emulate the exquisite art of procrastination. He must be imperturbable, able to receive bad news without manifesting displeasure, or to hear himself maligned and misquoted without the slightest twinge of irritation. His private life must be so ascetic as to give his enemies no opportunities to spread scandal. He must be tolerant of the ignorance and foolishness of his home government and know how to temper the vehemence of the instructions he receives. Finally, he should remember that overt diplomatic triumphs leave feelings of humiliation behind them and a desire for revenge: no good negotiator should ever threaten, bully or chide."

Perhaps, with some allowance being made for the technical and social changes of the last three centuries, this enumeration remains valid.

II COALITION DIPLOMACY

Earlier I expressed the view that policy making and policy management should be kept separate, that only the latter, strictly speaking, should be considered as diplomacy.

This is normally a good rule to follow, but there is one important qualification to be made to it. That qualification concerns the conduct of relations between governments inside a coalition. This requires diplomatic activity, of course, but it is of a special kind, covering negotiations and involving problems which often differ from those between states which have no special ties of alliance or association. This kind of coalition diplomacy, and this is contrary to what I have urged about other kinds, should not be separated from policy or conducted on too formal and professional lines.

It is concerned not so much with the negotiation of agreements as the working out of common policies for collective action inside agreements already made. It should be carried on in substantially the same way as discussions and negotiations between ministers inside a government. The North Atlantic Treaty Organization provides a good illustration of its operation — and absence.

There are, of course, many phases of the relations between NATO members, between the states of this embryonic Atlantic community, which should be conducted in the normal diplomatic way. But in the field of defense and foreign policy those relations, as I see it, should be centralized and coordinated in a mechanism which in some respects at least would serve the same purpose — and operate in the same way — as a cabinet does inside a democratic country.

We have such a mechanism now in the Permanent Council of NATO, which meets in Paris and on which every NATO member is represented. My criticism of this body is that its members, except at short and infrequent ministerial meetings, have been agents rather than principals in policy making; that it has, in other words, been too diplomatic and not enough political. This is, in fact, the exact reverse of the criticism that I have made earlier about other forms of diplomacy.

The essential purpose of the NATO Council should not be merely to replace the normal diplomatic machinery between the governments concerned by something more centralized, and therefore presumably more effective, but operating in the same way. It should be to make diplomacy in the formal sense entirely unnecessary by working out common policies in the fields of action covered by NATO, in the same way that policies are worked out by and become binding on all the members of a cabinet.

This cannot be done if the NATO Council is solely a formal diplomatic agency whose sovereign members merely exchange information about policy, instead of making it collectively, or who work together in drafting notes and communications that are to be sent by one or two of their governments to Moscow along lines previously determined by those governments.

Important changes in the right direction are now being made in the procedures and operation of the NATO Council, according to Paul Henri Spaak, the able and dynamic Secretary General of that organization. He had this to say on these matters in Boston on September 27, 1958: "It [NATO] is the very centre of the most significant diplomatic innovation ever attempted, and is not only creating new methods, but even a new spirit, where the relations of nations to each other are concerned. I can tell you today without disclosing any official secrets, that throughout the past year, the United States Government did not send the Soviet Government a single note on the proposed Summit Conference without first submitting it to the NATO Permanent Council . . . You will, I am sure, realize that this is an innovation, even a revolution in diplomatic practice. It is really extremely significant that the most powerful nation in the world should accept this form of consultation and adopt the new practice of inviting even the smallest of its allies to discuss with it, on a footing of complete equality, matters of mutual interest, and that in the vast majority of cases it should take account of suggestions it received. This is of cardinal importance if the Alliance is to live and develop. If successful this practice may well be the beginning of something very important and very new."

This is encouraging and, as Mr. Spaak says, of great importance, so far as it goes. But, to be effective, consultation should reach into the field of policy making as well as policy clearing.

This will not be easy, but it is essential, if NATO is to achieve that cohesion and unity in policy which is necessary for its survival. In a sense, it would be merely the extension into the international sphere of the habits and practices which are taken for granted in the operation of democratic government nationally. This broader international responsibility does not in any way remove or weaken the direct constitutional responsibility of a democratic government to its own people. It is something additional that has to be achieved. It is nothing that can be formalized, for it is more of a quality of outlook and will than a written commitment.

Such a requirement of united action based on a consensus of opinion inside the group will put a premium on those qualities of wisdom, patience, and foresight which any politician in a democracy needs if he is to stand firm on principle despite passing currents and passions of the moment. The Achilles' heel of despotism is its inability to understand the unconquerable instinct of the individual for freedom. That of a democratic coalition is the temptation to reject the requirements of collective action for the claims of national, short-run convenience or advantage.

Yet if we are to make a coalition work, if we are to operate successfully collective diplomacy, we must accustom ourselves to making and pursuing policy within a framework broader than that of our own country. This applies to the economic as well as to other aspects of policy. Attitudes to neighbors and allies cannot be kept in watertight compartments. Excessive economic nationalism, if unchecked, will sooner or later corrode and weaken any coalition and destroy cooperation and unity in foreign and defense policies.

Finally, those governments and peoples within our coalition whose strength gives them a position of leadership have a special obligation to cultivate the self-denying qualities of patience, restraint, and tolerance. In their turn, the smaller and less strong members will have to demonstrate, not a surrender of their identity or free judgment, which would be undesirable and impossible, but a sense of proportion and accommodation and a recognition that the responsibility of leadership and the possession of power do warrant special influence and weight in the counsels of the coalition.

Acceptance of the overriding claims of unity, and of

the delays and concessions which are sometimes necessary to cultivate it, comes hardest, of course, to the
strongest; for a consciousness of strength naturally
encourages self-confidence and is apt to induce a tendency to take for granted the acquiescence of others. The
less strong members of a coalition probably find it
easier than the stronger to be conscious of the anxieties
and attitudes of others, and easier also to recognize the
perils of disunity within the greater society of which
they form a part.

It was hoped — as I have indicated — that this objective of a coordinated and common policy could be
achieved through the use of the NATO Council. If,
however, this is to be done, the Council will have to be
given greater power and authority than it now pos-
sesses. It is true that there are periodic meetings of this
council when ministers, the policy makers, are present.
But these meetings are short, formal at times to the
point of being almost perfunctory, and often more concerned with private conversations, and with the council communiqué to follow, than with the hammering
out of a collective policy. I do not wish to depreciate
them. It is good and it is valuable for ministers of the
governments of a coalition to meet in this way and develop the practices, and even more important the habits,
of consultation. It would be even more useful if Council members with ministerial authority could meet con-

tinuously and thereby lift the NATO Council from the diplomatic to the political level.

I believe that the time has now come, both in order to facilitate the formation of an effective and united foreign policy, and for the development of Atlantic unity generally, to convert the NATO Council — or as many of its members as are willing to accept the obligations for united action involved — into a kind of political general staff, with greater power and authority than it now has. Today foreign policy and defense policy cannot be separated. Why then should their planning and coordination be separated.

I do not advocate, however, as has been proposed, the selection of a triumvirate of members with special responsibilities and privileges. The full council can always delegate authority to a smaller group for particular purposes. But delegation is not abandonment. Any arrangement by which three or four members would have the power and the right to commit the others would be quite impossible. It would make those others satellites or, at best, second-class members. No coalition of free sovereign states could operate on that basis, any more than it could on that of a mathematical majority of its members making decisions on the one state–one vote principle and empowered to take action in the name of all.

III NEGOTIATION AND DIPLOMACY

A most important if not *the* most important function of diplomacy, whoever practices it, career diplomats or foreign ministers, Communist dictators or Communist functionaries, is that of negotiation. Indeed, diplomacy is, in large part, the art of negotiation between governments, undertaken to further the interests of your own state, whether those interests are short-term or long-term, good or bad, peaceful or aggressive.

A sane and enlightened diplomacy, however, will always realize that in today's nuclear world where man now has the power of eliminating himself, national interests cannot any longer be separated from humanity itself. Indeed, by far the greatest national interest is, and must remain, the prevention of a war which would destroy humanity.

There never was a time in history when, for this supreme purpose, negotiation, through all the varied mechanisms of diplomacy, was more important, more difficult, and, at times, more frustrating. Negotiation, it should be remembered, means more than prepared monologues delivered at international congresses, or pronouncements at press conferences, or ex cathedra statements designed to frighten adversaries or impress reluctant allies.

Today, when the alternative to peace may be nuclear suicide, it is more important than ever to keep the channels of diplomacy open. Moreover, we should not be content merely to take advantage of any opportunities for negotiation that may arise. We should create such opportunities by a positive and dynamic diplomacy.

Centuries ago Cardinal Richelieu stood firm on a practice which is still good in 1959. Faced with what seemed to be a collapse of his policies, he refused to be discouraged. Instead, he became more determined than ever to go on negotiating without ceasing, openly or secretly, wherever and whenever possible, even though present results were negative and future ones were uncertain. Mr. John Foster Dulles gave expression to this idea in Washington early in 1958 to the National Press Club when he said: "Negotiation is one of the major tools of diplomacy. It would be the height of folly to renounce the use of this tool." One of our greatest dangers today is that in the face of the frustrations, obstacles, and setbacks we encounter in our efforts to negotiate with Communist states, we may throw away this tool, or become more and more reluctant to use it, or use it with hesitation and uncertainty.

The purpose and manner of negotiation is, in truth, as important an element in our strength — or our weakness — as military power or the lack of it. We often forget this. If our military weapons are out of date, if we rely on bayonets instead of missiles, we soon hear about it. There is a great public outcry, a demand to have the situation corrected and those who were responsible for it removed. If, however, our diplomatic objectives are mistaken or short-sighted, if our tactics are weak and fumbling, or rash and dangerous, there are ways and means of obscuring them or explaining them away. Curtains of iron, or velvet, or even words, can be drawn over diplomatic or political short-comings, whose effect therefore may not become known for a long time. Failures can even be converted by skilled publicity into what may seem to be successes. Negotiations conducted in public, in fact, by political personages are simply not permitted to fail — at least for some time.

This is one reason that diplomatic negotiations should normally be conducted in private.

I realize that it takes two to keep the process of a negotiation confidential, but there is no reason we should ever be the first to sin. If Moscow, by the crudity of some of its diplomatic techniques, by its strident and public appeal to peoples over the heads of their governments, makes confidential negotiation difficult or even impossible, we should on our side keep on trying to restore it to something which can facilitate constructive results. In any event, there is no excuse whatever for following such public polemical tactics in negotiations and discussions between friends and allies.

"All negotiations," wrote Alfred Duff Cooper in his memoirs, "whether concerning the sale of a horse or a proposal of marriage must be carried on confidentially." I agree, but with two reservations.

First, the policies which govern and guide negotiations should be publicly decided and publicly explained. There should be no secret commitments, specific or implied. The people who are asked to make the sacrifices, to man the barricades or die in the trenches when the breakdown of negotiation leads to war, have the right to know, and to approve or disapprove through their elected representatives, every commitment, every major policy that is proposed, and, indeed, every minor one that involves any kind of national obligation. There should be no secret diplomacy of that kind. In other words, the covenants should be open, as well as the policies on which they are based. But the detailed negotiations leading up to them need not be so.

The second reservation covers certain international situations concerning which negotiation can usefully be preceded by open conferences, conducted even with a maximum of publicity, so that international opinion, the international conscience, if you will, can be mobilized and brought to bear on a particular development with maximum impact.

This is especially true — and difficult — when international action is proposed in regard to developments which involve new problems and new ideas, where there are no precedents to guide and no disastrous experiences to avoid. Two such developments of grave significance are now facing us: the control of nuclear tests and the control of outer space. Here we have nothing to go on, but if we go wrong it could be fatal. We are entering new territory, in every sense of the word, when we begin public discussion of these subjects in such a world forum as the United Nations. Yet such discussion is important so that there might be the widest possible exchange of views on the principles involved and on the ideas that should govern later diplomatic negotiations with a view to seeking general international agreement.

This process of discussion has now begun with very limited positive results, though the obstacles in the way of agreement are at least being exposed.

The first and greatest of these obstacles is the relation to national security of both public discussion and private negotiation on these two subjects. It is quite impossible even to talk about the international legal concept of outer space or the technical aspects of nuclear tests without coming up against political and strategic considerations of paramount importance. This would be true even in the absence of international tension. It is dangerously obvious in an atmosphere of cold war, where security factors bedevil even the most general and exploratory discussions of these questions at any international assembly.

Their public consideration in a constructive manner is handicapped in another way. The search for a solution to the problems involved requires from expert advisers scientific knowledge possessed by only a few persons. Those few can often determine the principles to be adopted and the policies to be advanced because of the scientific advice they give. The political negotiator receiving such advice ignores it at his peril. But in considering it he must keep two things in mind. First, the scientific advice may come to him second-hand, screened by others, even other experts. Second, experts themselves often disagree, for instance over the radioactive effect of nuclear tests. Yet, if the negotiator or his government cannot be reasonably certain of the validity of the technical advice they receive, how can they possibly be sure that the political or diplomatic position they take is the right one.

It was not many years ago that the soldier or sailor could determine political developments by the technical military advice he gave, by the expert opinion he expressed on the consequences for national security of a particular course of political action. The chain of events leading up to the outbreak of war in 1914 is the classic example. Now the scientist, the nuclear physicist, the guided missile expert, shares and may soon dominate that role. His position, indeed, may be of greater importance in this respect than that of a chief of staff ever was, for two reasons.

One, the consequences of wrong scientific advice may now be more devastating because of our new weapons, which are themselves largely the achievement of the scientist. Two, a politician, such as Winston Churchill or Franklin D. Roosevelt, might feel that he knows quite as much about grand strategy as any military chief. He can hardly claim, however, to share the knowledge of a nuclear scientist, unless he happens — and this is rare enough — to be one himself.

Public discussion of diplomatic issues prior to negotiations is not always productive of good results. But, as I have said, there are occasions when it should be attempted; and there have been occasions when it has made subsequent agreement easier. The General Assembly of the United Nations has shown how this technique can be applied to clarify issues and mobilize international opinion, either as a prelude to negotiation or as the only possible substitute for negotiation when it is not possible.

Of course, the techniques of public discussion can also be used — as they have been at the United Nations and elsewhere — to becloud issues and frustrate negotiations. This, however, should not be allowed to conceal the present and even more the potential value of the United Nations as a world assembly for the public consideration on a universal basis of certain international issues prior to, and often as a foundation for, the negotiation of solutions.

It is not the idea or the procedure for such public international discussion which should be condemned and abandoned, but its abuse by government for obstructive and selfish purposes. That abuse is clear when governments drag tense and explosive situations for the wrong reasons before an international assembly where highly publicized and bad-tempered debate would be the worst possible prelude to negotiation and settlement.

Recent experiences show that the UN Assembly is being increasingly used for this purpose. It constitutes, indeed, its chief value for the Communist members, though they are not the only offenders. In present circumstances we must, in fact, expect such abuse of the Assembly by those totalitarian states which see in it, as they see in diplomacy and negotiation generally, an instrument of national policy rather than of international agreement.

Those members also who have recently emerged from colonial status, and who now constitute a sizable bloc, find it difficult to resist the temptation to use the assembly primarily for the expression of anti-imperialist feeling. This is certainly understandable, but it is often misdirected. Ignoring the fact that the kind of imperialism of which they have unhappy memories is dead or dying in the world, they aim their shafts at that target, and allow themselves to be exploited in the process by the only imperialism which is now an active and immediate menace to national freedom, the imperialism which is centered in Moscow and Peking.

The UN Assembly now has eighty-two members. It represents, with one very conspicuous exception, nearly all the nations of the world. As such it can be an accurate, if disturbing, reflector of world conflicts and tensions and hopes. It is the vivid and at times disturbing symbol of our interdependence. With all its faults and all its failures, it embodies that emerging sense of international community which stretches beyond nation and region and which is, after all, the only realistic concept in this nuclear age.

In the United Nations, governments have to parade not only words but policies before the scrutiny, friendly and unfriendly, of the international public. This important function of clarification, of analysis, of education, is taking place on every day that there is a United Nations meeting anywhere in the world. This is a kind of open diplomacy which can be healthy and good, just as its excesses — diplomacy by "loud speaker" or by insult — can be harmful and bad.

Unfortunately it is the destructive activity at the UN that gets the most publicity, the acid and acrimonious debate aimed not at assisting the search for a solution but at establishing your own innocence and the other side's guilt if that search fails. Debate of this kind lends itself to dramatization and exaggeration by those who are reporting it for public consumption. Conflict is always headline news. It needs no publicity agent. Peaceful and constructive achievement, however, often has no one to sing its praises.

In the abuse of the UN for unworthy publicity and propaganda purposes lies one of the greatest dangers for the future of the world organization. It is also one of the strongest arguments against unrestricted public international discussion of explosive issues. A harmful atmosphere can be created by excessive and distorted publicity. This may even be unintentional at times. But it is also often done with calculation by a dictator or a demagogue. He may deliberately stir up a breeze of opinion which he hopes will be a beneficent one wafting him to a diplomatic success. Publicity makes it a wind and he reaps the whirlwind. It is easy to stir up public opinion by speeches and pictures and radio harangues. It is equally easy to become its victim when the negotiation must begin, and when reason and understanding, having been undermined by propaganda, become overwhelmed by passion and prejudice.

The purpose of all diplomatic negotiation should be to reach agreement. This normally requires some adjustment of position on both sides. Such adjustment, however, is not made easier, and may become impossible, when every alteration of position, however slight, becomes headlined within the hour as appeasement (a good word gone wrong) or desertion of morality or the abandonment of principle. In negotiations of this kind, and in this atmosphere, the negotiator too often becomes the captive of his daily communiqué or, even more, of the headlines given to it. There is nothing much more futile than negotiation in which each side shoots communiqués at the other. They can't, of course, kill the negotiators, but they can kill the chances of agreement. Headlines too often merely harden convictions without clarifying them, for no political negotiator finds it easy to deny or dispute them.

The other course is infinitely to be preferred by the honest seeker after solutions: public discussion, nationally and internationally, of all the issues, but conducted with restraint and with a view to preparing the way for negotiation, which should be conducted through confidential diplomatic channels permitting of some ground for maneuver within principles and policies previously decided and made known.

Please do not misunderstand me. I do not advocate secret deals around green baize tables in a dim light with all the curtains drawn. No democratic state — as I have already said — can or should countenance commitments secretly entered into, or adopt policies or make engagements without the people knowing about them and the legislature passing on them.

But full publicity for objectives and policies and results does not mean, or at least should not mean, that
negotiation must always be conducted, step by step, in
public. Certainly no private activity, not even a public
relations business, could be operated successfully by
such methods. And government is today the most important and delicate activity of all. Negotiation in an
agitated gold-fish bowl, then, is often a serious obstacle
to the reaching of agreement.

There is another obstacle which, if not so obvious,
can be as formidable. My anxiety about its effect is
based on personal experience extending over many
years. This obstacle is carelessness in, or hostility to, the
recording of an agreement or an understanding.

There is nothing more important in negotiation than
to make it perfectly clear in unambiguous terms what
was agreed upon, whether the agreement was reached
formally or informally, specifically or by implication.
The lines should be made so clear that little or nothing can be read between or behind them. Precision and
clarity of this kind are often lamentably lacking today
in diplomatic documents.

The first requirement is to put your decision or your
understanding into written words. Particularly dangerous is the hurried meeting of foreign ministers,
without any document recording their conclusions,
each thinking he knows what was decided and each
giving to the world, in a press conference after a tiring

air trip, a version which, when read by the others, suggests that he may have been less than candid with them. This has caused trouble and misunderstanding among allies and has prejudiced subsequent cooperation between them. It weakens trust and good faith, which must be a foundation for friendly and constructive diplomatic cooperation.

Moreover, when talks are recorded in a document, it is essential, but it is not always done, that the document should be one agreed on by *all* the participants. There should not be separate official records, which can become a fertile field for later misunderstanding. Reluctance to follow this course is one of the results of the growth of ministerial, as opposed to professional, diplomatic negotiation. There are politicians who suspect the meticulously drafted document because of the limitations of its very precision.

Lloyd George, a great innovator and exponent of the art of political and personal diplomacy, was one of these. He did not believe in the careful recording by experts of negotiations, any more than he believed in conducting them through foreign offices and diplomatic representatives via letters and dispatches. "I wish the French and ourselves never wrote letters to each other," he said in 1920. "If you want to settle a thing, you should see your opponent and talk it over with him. The last thing you do is write him a letter." This is dangerous and confusing advice, as Lloyd George's own experience shows. His unrecorded conversations, often over the breakfast table, more than once led to commitments whose nature was unclear even to the participants and unknown to those who were supposed to carry them out.

This practice did not disappear with Lloyd George. Ramsay MacDonald, to cite another British example, was an enthusiastic practitioner of the unwritten and imprecise promise, while at one tragic moment in history, Neville Chamberlain thought that a scrap of political paper, hastily scribbled after a short personal discussion on the summit, had brought peace.

Some years later a French parliamentary commission, examining the reasons why it was not peace but a sword that emerged from Munich, had this to say in its report: "After the conclusion of the Treaties of 1919, ministers had the habit of multiplying their contacts with their colleagues in other countries. The abuse of direct conversation opens the door to numerous dangers. Engagements are taken too early. They are often improvised. It is better to define the course of a negotiation by a note which has matured in the silence of the ministry than by chance exchanges which are likely to be imprecise." These are wiser words than those of Lloyd George.

Even when you have a note, memorandum, communiqué, or treaty covering everything that was done, and agreed to by all, subsequent difficulty and misunderstanding can be caused by different meanings given to certain words in agreed texts. There can be various reasons for this.

The first involves difficulties in translation. Words which mean one thing in English may, without great care in translation, become something else, say, in French, where no great damage may ensue between friends, or in Russian, with more unfortunate results. Sometimes the misconstruction given to translated words is deliberately mischievous; in other cases it is quite innocent. This is something that should never be forgotten, especially in negotiation with Russians, whose rigidity about words is increased by a deep suspicion of the way we use them — a suspicion which, I fear, is mutual.

A second reason, which has nothing to do with translation, is an inability, due very often simply to an inadequate basic education, to find the right words to express meaning. I know that there have been occasions, and I have been concerned with one or two, when, as the lesser of two evils, words were used in recording the results of negotiations or discussion whose value lay precisely in the fact that they were imprecise, that they could be interpreted somewhat freely and therefore could be used not so much to record agreement as to conceal a disagreement which it was desired to play down and which, it was hoped, would disappear in time. It is a practice, however, which is only rarely justified.

There is another reason for these drafting difficulties: time, or rather the lack of it; time to search for the right words which would never leave any room for doubt as to exactly what was agreed on. In earlier days of the carriage and four, and the quill pen, the negotiators had ample time to make sure that if and when they agreed, such agreement was embodied in words the meaning of which was understood by all concerned. The modern diplomatic negotiator has no such advantage. He arrives by air. He has three days before he has to leave by air. He works to a deadline as well as for a headline. As a consequence, texts are rushed through, ambiguities are overlooked, so that the plane can be caught for the next conference or for a meeting with the external affairs committee of the legislature or for a speaking engagement at a Shriners' convention five thousand miles away.

I have seen this frenzied process at work in conferences, and I know that it can cause trouble even between friendly governments, as all hasty and sloppy work can cause trouble. In short, the ambiguities of carelessly recorded negotiations create the misunderstandings that can frustrate the most carefully conceived policies.

There is another factor which has a bearing on this

special problem. If you are not clear in your ideas, you are not likely to be clear in their expression. It is, or it should be, therefore, a first principle of diplomatic negotiation that you are certain about your own objectives.

You may feel that in laboring these points, too much publicity and not enough precision, I am paying too much attention to the trivia of diplomatic activity. But I assure you that trivia can make trouble. I agree, however, that the techniques of negotiation are not so important as the desire and will to settle problems by discussion and agreement, as well as a clear understanding of the real nature of the problems to be settled.

I have mentioned some difficulties facing the diplomatic negotiator which are of general application. But there are special difficulties, and even risks, in negotiating with Communists, of either the Russian or Chinese variety.

We know, from experience, that the Soviet doctrine of "competitive coexistence" assumes a competition in which they observe no rules but their own and obey no referee but their own. Soviet Russia certainly owes none of its successes in negotiation, and need attribute none of its failures, to the playing fields of Eton. Its methods are crudely practical, coldly pragmatic — unyielding, obstinate, and ill-mannered. In the policy which it defends and the interests it advances, Soviet diplomacy admits no obligation to its own people except insofar as they are the ingredients of state or party power. It admits also no obligation to the future except as an extension in time and an increase in magnitude of that power. All this may put Western policy and diplomacy at a temporary disadvantage. But it is one which we can overcome, especially if we know the nature of the system we are up against, and are clear about our own purposes. It is, in fact, even more important to be clear about what is in our own mind than to speculate about or try to discover what is in the other person's.

This brings me to another advantage that the Soviets often have in negotiation. They are usually clear about their objectives, and this, as I have already said, is a major prerequisite to successful negotiation and consistent policy. Just as today Russia's first objective in an attack would be clearly to destroy Western capacity to retaliate, so its major objective in diplomacy, in my view, is to lessen and then eliminate the influence of the United States in Asia and Africa, to divide and then isolate the United States from its allies. The USSR and international Communism would then sweep, though not necessarily by arms, through the whole world. This is what Mr. Khrushchev meant, and not, I think, nuclear war, by his notorious cocktail party observation, "We shall bury you." There is no doubt that he and his colleagues are confident and convinced about the triumph of their system in this struggle for supremacy.

Are we as clear and confident about our own objectives?

As our society is free, these objectives are bound to be more complex, less coherent perhaps, than those of a totalitarian state. Nor can they ever be divorced from moral considerations, either genuine or occasionally contrived. These factors may raise obstacles in achieving clarity and certainty in our objectives, but they do not affect the importance and value of such clarity in the pursuit of policy.

Sir Harold Nicolson was right when he wrote that "the essence of a good foreign policy is certitude." But he was also right when he emphasized that this is not easy to achieve in a democratic state, where opposition in press and parliament is less likely to concentrate against an elastic than against a precise foreign policy. This elasticity, as it happens, often conforms to the needs and advantages of domestic political exigencies. It therefore may make the expression of a vague but idealistic purpose or principle preferable to a concrete statement of policy. It is always safe, and usually popular, to make ringing declarations against sin and for international morality. It is often less safe, and less popular, to be clear and precise on the policy to be followed in respect of a specific issue.

Prudence may dictate platitudes. Votes may counsel vagueness. But not always. At times the reverse may happen. Public opinion may swing passionately, or its leaders may swing passionately, behind a particular course of action or policy. Here there may be too much certainty, too much strong, straight talk in pursuit of a wrong objective.

In such circumstances, when opinion has come down passionately, if not permanently, on a particular side of a particular question of foreign policy, the danger is that negotiation may become too much a matter of hewing to a particular line, holding to it with bold and sweeping and unconditional statements. When an issue is considered by public opinion solely in terms of black and white, then dogmatic and precise statements, and not the vague declarations that I have just been mentioning, will be politically popular and therefore alluring to the political negotiator. In yielding to this form of temptation, however, he may find later that he has painted himself, colorfully but unhappily, into a diplomatic corner.

All this means that it is not wise in diplomatic negotiation to allow that clarity about objectives which is necessary, to degenerate into rigidity and inflexibility of method, without any ground being left for maneuver and for change.

What, then, *are* our objectives?

The primary one, and we must keep repeating it

again and again, is peace, based on friendly, constructive and cooperative relations between all peoples. Such
an objective means far more than the singularly sterile
and meaningless concept of "coexistence".

Western democratic governments have no aggressive
or imperialist designs. This is as true of the most powerful, the United States of America, as it is of, say, Uru-
guay or Iceland. Indeed, Americans, though no Russian may believe it, are perhaps the least imperialisti-
cally minded people that ever achieved great power in
the world. Bringing the legions back to Idaho or Ore-
gon or Massachusetts would evoke nothing but cheers
among the legionnaires and their leaders, if it could
safely be done. Americans are not by nature or desire
wandering empire builders. The "white man's burden"
has little appeal for them, and the call of far places can
be satisfied on their own continent. Nor do economic
pressures drive them overseas. They are home-
bodies, and their "westerns" give them an adequate if
vicarious sense of adventure.

They are, however, generous and outpouring and
sentimental. They are natural givers and their sym-
pathies are easily stirred. Above all, they like to be
liked. But they have not yet learned that national generosity, however great and whole-souled, when associated with power and wealth does not usually result in gratitude, especially if it becomes confused with
international political and strategic considerations. A

giant can achieve recognition and respect, but not often affection, or always understanding. This is something that the giant has to accept, or his policy is likely to be swayed too much by emotion of one kind or another.

All history shows this to be the case, and most recently, the history of the British Empire. Some time ago a British subject, Mr. Eugen Weber, teaching at the University of Iowa, made some witty and perceptive reflections on this matter. I would like to quote two paragraphs:

"The Greeks despised the Romans as Barbarians; no doubt the Egyptians in their turn despised the Greeks. We British have also had our time of greatness — our time of world supremacy. What were we in those days? We were perfidious Albion. We were a nation of long-toothed milords; of lean and angular spinsters; patronizing Cook's tours, gaping at European culture (which we were not supposed to understand); and calling loudly wherever we went for tea and porridge. Now we are decaying, and only the memories of this great tradition still live on. We have gathered the distinction of decay. People prize us, like one of the riper sorts of cheese. We are supposed to enshrine and guard admirable traditions, a great cultural heritage, which no one seemed to suspect (or at any rate admit) a generation or two ago. It is wonderful what a little failure can do!

"Meanwhile, the Americans have taken over, more

nilly than willy, the banner with the strange device of the white man's burden. They provide the perfidy, they provide the comic relief, they provide the gaping, un-cultured tourists chewing gum and sipping cokes. They are the powerful and the rich, and for this they must pay the penalty; and one part of the penalty is that they cannot be loved when they are feared — or ex-ploited." This, however, is a diversion.

If peace is the primary purpose of our policy, closely allied to that purpose, indeed part of it, should be the use of diplomacy for the easing of tension in the world. Such easing of tension not only makes for peace, it also makes sense in terms of *Realpolitik*. In such an easier and more relaxed political climate, divisions and con-tradictions inside the Communist camp can be most surely and effectively exposed. Freedom will have a better chance to grow and triumph, for national despotism is in greatest danger when the international atmosphere is calm.

We seek, then, peace and the easing of tension; co-operation for good purposes between all states; free-dom for all peoples with security and responsibility.

To achieve these objectives, our diplomacy must be as effective as our armed strength. It must display initiative and imagination and constructive purpose. We must act more so that we will have to react less. We must avoid — and here we have not been very suc-cessful — being forced on the defensive. As Henry A.

Kissinger has said in a recent edition of *Foreign Affairs:* "One of the difficulties the free world has had in dealing with the Soviet bloc is that we have been clearer about the things we oppose than those we stand for. This has given much of our negotiations with the Soviet Union the quality of a stubborn rear-guard action designed primarily to thwart Soviet overtures. It has enabled the Soviet leadership to define the issues in international debate, putting us in the position of respondent rather than initiator. World-wide pressures are built up against us before we have a chance to demonstrate our own purposes and values." This is very true and very important.

I realize how easy it is to become both fearful and discouraged in negotiation; how tempting it is to take the path of least resistance, to abandon both initiatives and risks for peace, to dig ourselves deeper and deeper into our trenches, waiting for the inevitable but hoping to prevent it by piling up nuclear weapon on nuclear weapon. In such circumstances our posture (that seems to be the current word) will, I admit, be formidable, but it may be frozen. We may become firmly fixed to positions once taken, hoping for the best while fearing the worst. We may indeed become so deeply rooted that we can't adapt ourselves to changing conditions. Once we get into that position, we are in danger of defeat.

Our diplomacy must be based, of course, on strength,

but, as I shall later try to show, on a strength which is greater than military, and on principles which need not include a sanctimonious morality that arrogates all virtue unto itself.

It must also be imbued with patience which will not be weakened either by discouragement or provocation. This means refusing to throw in our hands at the first rebuff, taking the long-term as opposed to the short-term view of our interests and the problems that affect them.

With patience there must be steadiness, a refusal to be carried away by elation at some successful achievement or to be thrown into jitters and despair by some reverse. It is as foolish to be panicked by a Sputnik or a Lunik as it would be to be overcome by jubilation if we reached the moon first.

I know how difficult it is to keep an even keel on a stormy sea. But it is all the more important just because the sea *is* stormy. In this respect, Western negotiators, as I have already pointed out, have some short-run disadvantages compared with their Communist counterparts. Our public opinion is free and therefore in the short run can be mercurial and unstable, and at times blown about. But if policy makers and diplomatic agents take every shift in domestic opinion as a major change of front, there will be continual unsteadiness, and success in the difficult and delicate work of negotiation will be hard indeed to win.

We will not, furthermore, have this essential steadiness unless we accept the fact that there are not going
to be easy and quick solutions to our "cold war" international problems. Some of them, indeed, admit
of no solution at all in present circumstances. Yet this
should not unduly alarm or excite us. Time may take
care of them, as it has so often done in history, until we
learn to live with them without too much trouble. But
time may need assistance now and then from us; otherwise it will not be on our side, even if we are angels!

If some problems, in present circumstances, should
at present be left alone, there are others that with patience and perseverance can be solved even with Communists. We should realize, however, that this will not
be done either by sentimentalizing or by slugging, but
only through hard-headed, realistic negotiation in order to find agreement in each case on a basis of mutual
self-interest. In present circumstances, no higher level
of agreement than this is likely to be reached, either
that of friendly cooperation or of any common purpose. But it will do, until we can reach a higher and
better level, that of good will.

There are, of course, many other useful rules to follow as we search for security by negotiation. We should
not permit the Communists to drag us down to their
level of debate and dialectic. In discussion we should
not mistake vilification for vigor, or sound and fury for
sense and firmness. We would also be wise, I think, to

follow the advice of a distinguished former United States delegate to the United Nations, Senator Warren Austin, when he said, "Always leave your adversary room to retreat." That seems to me to make sense, if not in war, at least in negotiation, and even with Communists.

Finally, we should resist the Anglo-Saxon tendency to make a moral issue of every political problem. There are bound to be some that can safely and honorably be dealt with on the basis of political expediency, while others involve moral principles which should not be betrayed. It is essential, though often difficult, to learn to recognize the distinction between them. We will never do so if we assume that every position we take, or have been maneuvered into taking, against a Communist government is one which is automatically based on a morality from which there can be no retreat or on which there can be no compromise.

There are issues and occasions, of course, when a man or a nation "must decide, in the strife of truth with falsehood, for the good or evil side." But there are others when the moral position is not so clear-cut, or the right side so easy to find, except for those who have already taken sides on every issue in advance, and who consider that all who are with them are saints and all the others irredeemable sinners. The identification of every political step we take with morality is a form of self-righteousness that we should try to avoid.

If, for instance, we base our opposition to the use
of force by a Communist government, which is powerful and aggressive and to be feared, on moral principles which admit of no compromise or concession,
then equally to be opposed as immoral is the use of any
force for national purpose by any non-Communist
despotism which we do not fear and which might even
be on our side in the cold war.

We can get ourselves into some queer contradictions
on this score. Power politics and defense strategy cannot always be explained or defended satisfactorily in
moral terms. We of the West lay ourselves open to the
charge of hypocrisy when we try to do so. So we should
not assume that because an ally is anti-Communist he
is *ipso facto* a good democrat and therefore a member
in good standing of what we at times, somewhat carelessly, call the "free world." If anti-Communism were
enough, Hitler would be the greatest and the most sin-
cere crusader for freedom in our time.

There may be occasions when alliances have to be
formed with governments which are totalitarian but
not aggressive. Let us not confuse the issue by assuming
that when we support them against Communist governments, we are doing so on moral and ideological
grounds. The situation concerning the islands of
Quemoy and Matsu provides one, but only one, example of what I mean. These islands, within Chinese
territorial waters, are in dispute between two Chinese

governments. One is a Communist despotism and, with the Soviet Union behind it (whether pushing or being pulled, I do not know), represents, in the eyes of many people in more than one nation, a threat to the American and to the whole non-Communist position in the western Pacific.

It is natural, then, that the United States should support, for reasons which need have nothing directly to do with democracy, the Chinese Nationalist government on Formosa. If that island were attacked, whether from Peking or any place else, this might well be aggression requiring collective action for defense, because Formosa is not necessarily a part of continental China. But if the offshore islands are attacked by one side in the Chinese civil war and defended by the other, the situation is very different. No question of principle arises which in my view requires support for the Chinese Nationalist government in such a conflict.

It has been said that force must always be resisted. But if force were to be resisted in every civil war by the United States supporting one side and the USSR the other, peace would soon become even more precarious than it is at present. Such a doctrine seems to me to be a dubious and even dangerous basis for diplomacy in China, in the Middle East, or even in Latin America.

It has also been said that these Chinese offshore islands are now important, perhaps essential, to the defense of Formosa. If that is true, it is because Chiang

Kai-shek has made them so by a planned transfer of one-third of his troops to them from Formosa. It was, I think, bad diplomacy which allowed that to happen. Even in the most extreme acceptance of the necessity of standing firm against any use of Communist power, or threat thereof, surely a less exposed and more secure position, strategic and political, could have been found. Nor do I admit that those who feel this way on this issue should be considered as lacking in principle or in firmness.

Perhaps, with the display of United States power in the area, the situation may quiet down again as it did early in 1955. If it does, surely this time advantage should be taken of the lull, as we were led to expect it would be taken last time, so that Quemoy and Matsu can be made again tactically unimportant for the defense of Formosa by the return of the Chinese troops on them to that island, where they would be serving an important and genuine defensive purpose.

IV POWER AND DIPLOMACY

I have been stressing the importance of diplomacy and negotiation in the pursuit of policy. Yet, however good and wise it may be, diplomacy in our imperfect world is not likely to be effective unless there is power behind it. Strength without skilled diplomatic direction may lead you straight against a stone wall. But diplomacy, without strength behind it, may be merely an aimless exercise.

I have said, for instance, that I did not think it was wise policy to have permitted so much of the armed strength of Nationalist China to be concentrated on two islands just off the coast. Nevertheless, I admit that there would be little possibility of altering that policy in the right direction without disaster, or indeed of accomplishing anything at all, if the United States did not possess great strength in this area.

The situation today in Berlin is another illustration of both the value and the limitation of power behind policy. If the governments concerned, and they should certainly include all the NATO powers, do not oppose Russian arbitrary demands for withdrawal from Berlin with the firmness which requires power to make it ef-

fective, and the unity which is almost as essential, then
they will suffer a serious defeat, whose consequences
will extend far beyond Berlin. But force and firmness
alone will not solve this problem. The Western powers
should couple their resolution with proposals of their
own which might form the basis of a settlement more
enduring than the one made in 1945 in the forcing circumstances of war. If they do not, any success they may
now achieve by opposing power with power will surely
be short-lived.

It is the relation between these two things — power
and policy — which is vital. When that relation is a
good and a balanced one, it can be described as power
politics of the right kind. Such politics are often taken
to mean the use of power for aggressive and wrong purposes. But they can mean not only the politics of not
being overpowered, but also the use of power construc-
tively to back up policies and negotiations whose object
is to reduce the possibility of having to use such
power in the future.

The problem is essentially a matter of a balanced
and stable relation. If we pile up arms unnecessarily
high every time there is a crisis, or even when there is
not; if we brandish them belligerently every time there
seems to be a threat; or, on the other hand, if we throw
them aside to save money as soon as a particular crisis
is over, or a particular threat is removed, then we will
not succeed in our policy and our diplomacy or de-

serve to. This is where wisdom should enter, in the way we collect and use force, steadily and carefully, as a backing for a peacemaking diplomacy.

Closely connected with, indeed a part of, the relation between power and policy which I have mentioned, is that between power and security.

All history shows that security — or peace — cannot for long be guaranteed merely by superiority in arms. The attempt to do so inevitably provokes countermeasures on the part of those against whom you arm, which in turn makes an even greater effort on your part necessary. The vicious circle of fear and arms, insecurity and more arms begins, and the ending cannot be a happy one even when it is not disastrous.

In present circumstances, this reliance on power for security means suspension between uneasy peace and global war, in a state of tension and fear, with two great agglomerations of world power facing each other in bitter hostility across a gulf of misunderstanding and ignorance. This is our present and unhappy position. What we face in such a situation is, at best, continuing conflict short of war, with occasional limited wars kept short of the ultimate catastrophe of a global holocaust by the fear of mutual annihilation.

Peace, that is the absence of nuclear war, is now balanced precariously on the knife-edge of terror, and the outer spaces are becoming cluttered up with satellites which may now carry only dogs, monkeys, and delicate bits of apparatus but which will soon be able to carry nuclear warheads designed not to stay up with the stars above but to crash down upon us mortals below who have contrived such fearsome and wonderful devices. Our immediate and temporary protection from these grim consequences of our own genius requires the possession of overwhelming, totally destructive power. That is the "deterrent" which we hear so much about: total power, the ultimate in material strength, embodied in a hydrogen bomb or missile.

The possession of this kind of force may, I admit, be an effective present deterrent against attack. Its use is also an assurance of the destruction of yourself as well as the enemy. Hence, if both sides have this power and cannot be prevented from using it in retaliation against an attack, then neither side will dare use it. It becomes sterilized and, paradoxically, the object of policy and even strategy is to keep it so. For this purpose, it is the primary and overriding purpose of defense planning to ensure enough warning to get your own retaliatory forces, missiles or aircraft, into the air before they are destroyed. Otherwise the deterrent would cease to deter.

This is a situation which is, I think, quite unprecedented in history. True, back in earliest times, if a tribe used force against the tribe in the next valley — perhaps the two of them constituted their "one world" of that day — and was defeated, its members were exterminated or enslaved. But the victors, at least, survived and gained supremacy by their victory. Therein lies the difference with 1959 and the possible use of unlimited nuclear power to settle tribal or, if you like, global disputes.

War may have once been the pursuit of policy by other means, just as in the Communist world today policy may be the waging of war by other means. None of this makes any sense, however, when applied to allout nuclear war, which cannot mean the triumph of policy if it also means total and general destruction.

Therefore, I repeat, such nuclear power is unlikely to be used at present by one side so long as it can also be used by the other. This, however, does not solve the problem of security. A type of surprise nuclear attack by missiles from the air or under the water may soon be practicable (there are those who say it already is) which could knock out most or all of the retaliatory forces before they could be launched. The possibility of doing this would be a strong temptation to an aggressor to strike swiftly and without warning in the hope of escaping the counterblow.

Even if this thesis is dismissed as unrealistic, and even if the aggressor could not secure immunity from a smashing counterblow, and he knows it, a tragic miscalculation of consequences might result ultimately in a use of total power which was not intended when the first move was made. A chain reaction might be set up leading from a bullet to an ICBM. We might slide rather than jump into the abyss. This, in fact, is now our greatest danger. Sound policy and wise diplomacy is a far better protection against it than more H-bombs.

Russian leaders show signs of a cold and realistic awareness of this situation. They are likely to relate the decision to use force to the risk of survival. I believe that they will draw back if and when that risk becomes clear. But this only underlines the danger of miscalculation. We in the democracies seem to approach the problem from the opposite side. We assume that overwhelming national force can be used only when the issue *is* one of survival.

Total power, then, may be necessary as a deterrent against large-scale aggression. But it has no other political security or value. Yet this weapon, the effectiveness of which depends on its non-use, is the one which now commands most public support in the United States, the leader of the Western alliance. So we keep on becoming more and more powerful in the weapons we can't use — except for deterrence. How far do you have to go before deterrent power is sufficient to deter? If you go further, the additional power is not only unnecessary and wasteful, but more weapons on the other side cancel out your own increased power, and both sides are merely wasting money, energy, and power itself.

What tragic and stupid folly! It makes one believe
that Bernard Shaw was right when he said: "If the
other planets are inhabited" — and we'll find that out
soon — "they must think of earth as their lunatic asy-
lum."

I have been talking about the necessity and the limitations of nuclear power. Its possession by one country
has, of course, results that now extend far beyond national boundaries. Both the reassurance and the fear it
creates include all nations on either side of the cold war,
or indeed on no side.

Power on your side, even outside your own national
control, may no longer intimidate you. You may worry
about the way it is being used in pursuit of policy
against the other side, but you have no fear that it will
ever be used against you. The growth of American na-
val power once caused fear in London. Its overwhelming character now brings comfort, and "Rule, Britan-
nia" is sung when an American nuclear submarine puts
into a British port.

The United States a few years ago was the only
country in the non-Communist world in the possession
of a hydrogen bomb, but when the United Kingdom
tested one successfully, it was welcomed into the inner
circle by the country that the United Kingdom could
now devastate with its new weapons. This merely shows
that power is not fearful when policy does not make it

so. Conflict may have become bipolarized in the world, but at least the area of mutual confidence has been enlarged. This, perhaps, is a form of progress.

If the danger, however, as I hold it to be, is now not so much from the calculated use of all-out nuclear power as from accidental conflict or from a limited and peripheral conflict which might spread, where do power and policy enter here? What kind of armed strength should be maintained to meet the danger? What kind of diplomacy to remove it?

Certainly nuclear weapons of mass destruction — the "deterrent" — provide no solution to this problem of accidental or limited war. Indeed, if that were our only answer, the Western coalition would be in a bad way, strategically and politically. If there is a relatively small-scale aggression against an ally, involving only the use of conventional, or at worst tactical atomic weapons, is this to be met with nuclear strategic retaliation by the United States? If so, does this mean that our defense strategy is now such as to convert every war in the NATO area into a world nuclear war, in the hope that the certainty of this result will prevent any war? This is certainly playing for the highest stakes.

Is the awful choice, no action or total action; sudden destruction or slow defeat; conventional conquest or nuclear suicide? The answer must be no. There must be some other course, some other alternative than this.

Perhaps it may be found, not in discarding the capacity for total retaliation, which would be folly, but in preventing that capacity from getting out of hand while developing another military deterrent against limited war through a balance on another level which would make massive strategic retaliation unnecessary except in the case of a major, all-out aggression.

There is no other way of finding this balance, this other deterrent, than that of collective action for defense on the part of those who are willing to band together for such action. It is the only defense that makes any sense. It is as important in support of policy as the multiplication of megaton bombs and missiles. It requires also, as I have tried to show, unity in other things than defense.

So long as the NATO alliance is weak in conventional power, and in the unity which would make it effective, the alternative is to rely excessively on those unlimited weapons, such as H-bombs, unsuitable for defense except in one contingency and, in any case, completely outside collective control. The greater this reliance, the more difficult it becomes to find the resources and the resolve to develop through NATO other forms of conventional defense as a deterrent. So one or two members of the coalition push their nuclear power and strategy even further. There then develops another chain reaction which may end by weakening the coalition and making impossible collective defense.

If the other members of the Atlantic Alliance feel—

as many of them do and with some reason — that their only real defense is now the U.S. Strategic Air Force, the hydrogen bomb, and the ICBM, they will become less and less concerned with making the effort and the sacrifice required for their own defense by other means. Ultimately, they will also lose interest in NATO as an agency for collective defense and collective policy. There are signs that this feeling is already developing.

It is then of great importance, both for military and for political reasons, to get away from this "all or nothing" concept as the only way of establishing a balance between power and policy, or power and security. It will require the build-up within the coalition of mobile, hard-hitting, balanced collective forces, which will be a deterrent against limited attack and effective for defense against such attack, if it occurs, without the use of nuclear weapons of mass destruction.

There is another kind of force, also limited in character, which in certain circumstances could be of great importance in support of policy and diplomacy. In the long run it provides, in fact, our best hope to this end because it is supranational in concept and control. It is an international police and peace-insuring force, used as an instrument of the international community, after a United Nations decision authorizing such use. I think of four occasions during the last twenty-five years when hopes mounted high that peace might be secured, or at least strengthened, through international force behind international decisions.

The first of these occurred in the mid-thirties when the League of Nations was dealing with the Abyssinian crisis, when sanctions were voted against the adjudged aggressor. No one who was at Geneva then will ever forget the dramatic moment when the Foreign Minister of Great Britain pledged his government to "steady and collective resistance to aggression" and asked the other members to follow that course into the future with determination and resolve. This resolve, however, soon became "sicklied o'er" with fear and eventually disappeared in bickering and futility. The members of the League retreated from their high endeavor, destroyed any hope for effective collective action, and by so doing made certain, I believe, the war of 1939. The sad epilogue to that tragedy was a courageous little emperor pleading for justice at Geneva to an indifferent assembly as he went into exile.

There was a second chance at San Francisco in 1945. Once again we were led high by hope, and for a few brief but brilliant days felt that perhaps this time we had learned the lesson of the horrors and tragedies of our earlier failure, and that international cooperation with police force behind law might be achieved to save the world from another such scourge. Then the icy winds of enmity and fear began to blow and froze that vision into the hard and cruel reality of the cold war.

There was a third occasion when the Security Council of the United Nations, fulfilling the purposes of the Charter, invoked military sanctions against the aggressor in Korea. That decision, however, was only possible because the fortuitous absence of the Soviet representative — which is not likely to be repeated again in such circumstances — gave the Council immunity from his veto. The action in Korea, while a United Nations one in initiation and authority, was not broadly based internationally in control, organization, and participation. It was inevitable, and not open to criticism under the circumstances, that the United States should exercise a dominant influence on events, in a way which made this operation not the best model for any similar international initiative in the future. It did show, however, what the Security Council of the United Nations could do in the face of aggression if there were only essential unity among its members.

The last instance of UN action of this kind took place in 1956, during the Suez crisis, when the United Nations through its Assembly, and not the Security Council which had been made impotent by the veto, intervened to stop an armed conflict. It was a critical time, with Egyptian and Israeli forces in conflict and British and French forces having intervened militarily to bring that conflict to an end. The intervention, however, caused dangerous international repercussions.

The British and French governments had said that if the UN would take over the policing of the area and the separation of the forces of Israel and Egypt, they would withdraw. If this could not be done, the future looked dark for peace. Asia and Africa were bitter and angry and the Soviet Union only too happy to exploit these feelings for its own purposes.

Could the UN act in time? Could it act at all?

There was no precedent for any such police and peace action organized and directed by the UN Assembly. It was ill-prepared to take on this unexpected responsibility. But within a very few days a United Nations Emergency Force was in being, resolutions governing its use had been passed by the Assembly, offers of men had been made by more than a dozen states. In a few weeks an efficient, well organized force of high morale and purpose, serving under the blue flag of peace of the UN, was standing guard on the danger line. This made possible the withdrawal of national forces from the zone. Since then, and with the approval of the governments concerned, a cease-fire has been policed and there has been no shooting. Who can say that this action may not have prevented a local conflict from deteriorating into a major war?

It has been a heartening and hopeful experiment in peace preserving, in international organization, in the use of international force, and in effective and constructive diplomatic negotiation through the United Nations. Nor would it have been possible without the great skill, patience, and determination of the Secretary-General of the United Nations, who, during these weeks, broke new ground in diplomacy.

It is unwise, however, to exaggerate the meaning of what was done at this time. Success was only partial and limited. UNEF was not the kind of force visualized in the charter under the authority of the Security Council which would be strong enough to impose the will of the United Nations on a national government. A force like UNEF could do nothing to prevent a direct and naked aggression by a big or even a middle power which was determined to move. It probably would not be able to operate in the territory even of a small power, if that power objected, unless the great powers were in agreement to exert the necessary pressure.

Nevertheless, the events of Suez showed that in certain circumstances a United Nations force could be effective in securing an armistice, in pacifying a disturbed border, in helping to prevent brush fires from spreading. Nor can there be anything much more important than this, at a time when the greatest danger that faces us, I repeat, is not so much calculated, all-out nuclear aggression as a limited conflict, begun by accident or miscalculation, which would generate a chain-reaction ending in a hydrogen bomb.

Yet the truth remains that this first experience of a fully international peace force backing international diplomacy will have no permanent effect, that its value will be dissipated and lost, unless the members of the United Nations build a permanent structure on the foundation laid. This would mean creating a small permanent staff organization at New York to which the members of the UN — except the permanent members of the Security Council — would earmark trained and equipped police contingents to be used on the decision of the UN. This would be a far-reaching and important step. There is no indication, however, that the members of the UN are willing to take it. The half-hearted and timid action of the 1958 Assembly in considering the matter shows that narrow, short-sighted counsels may prevail and that nothing may be done. International force behind international decisions is still a far-distant dream to haunt men's minds, and only after disaster to stir their imaginations into fleeting and insufficient effort. Perhaps we are making some progress away from international anarchy and war, but time now moves very fast and who can say it is on the side of those men and forces that make for peace.

Military power, then, used wisely and with an understanding of its limitations, is an essential support for policy. But sound policy and astute diplomacy are themselves as much a source of strength as military power. The two are, in fact, and this has been the central thesis of these lectures, interrelated and interdependent. This is especially true at a time when nuclear developments dominate so much of our strategic and diplomatic thinking and planning.

There are also sources of power other than diplomacy and arms which are essential to the support of policy. Stalin showed a total unawareness of the nature and meaning of strength when, so the story goes, he equated its possession by the Pope to the number of divisions under the command of His Holiness. He was not the first despot in history — nor will he be the last — to make such a mistake, to ignore or underestimate the nonmilitary sources of power. An idea about to be born, or a currency about to be debased, can be as important for power or the loss of it as a hundred of Stalin's divisions.

Outside the area of bayonets and bombs, for instance, is the power that comes from an expanding and well-managed economy, from a stable and sturdy financial, industrial, and trading structure. In fact, this kind of strength, in the nuclear age, is absolutely essential for the arms themselves which are required. It can also be weakened by an excessive diversion of national effort and national resources to the acquisition of those arms. Here, again, it is all a matter of balance.

Without a flourishing and healthy national trade and investment base, strength, however expressed, will be limited in scope and nature. Without strong and expanding international trade and investment, the materially underdeveloped countries, now on the march politically, and impatient to make up for lost time, will never establish such a base. Yet it is vital that they do so, if international conflict is to be avoided and their increasing populations are not to result in social collapse. The magnitude of this problem can easily be seen when we realize that while it has taken two hundred million years to produce two and a half billions of people on this planet, it will take only the next forty years to double that number.

This is only one reason why we should help these emerging underdeveloped countries, by trade and aid. The use of our economic strength and resources in this way — but without political strings attached — can be an important adjunct to a positive and constructive diplomacy. I wish that we had been wiser and more imaginative in its use in recent years, that we could learn the lesson that generosity is not enough and that purpose and procedure in this matter are quite as important as policy.

The Soviet Union is becoming more and more conscious of the value of economic power to be used not only for national but for international political purposes, especially in its relations with underdeveloped countries. Nor are those relations greatly influenced, as those of the capitalist democracies are bound to be, at least on the trade side, by commercial considerations. It is enough to quote Khrushchev's remark to a group of visiting United States Congressmen in 1955 when he said: "We value trade least for economic reasons and most for political purposes." Trade and aid are, to Soviet negotiators, as much an element of diplomacy as military power, in their effort to achieve a single objective, the triumph of their own system throughout the world.

Yet they have been more successful in concealing this fact than has the United States, which has done so much more to assist other countries. Particularly in those countries uncommitted in the cold war, the American assistance program has often been received with a suspicion that does not seem to be attached to moves that the Soviet Union makes in this field. This may be partly due to a certain ineptness in methods and planning which The United States' aid activities have shown at times, and a corresponding carefulness and skill on the part of Communist operations. When there have been mistakes of this kind Communists have always been zealous and clever in distorting and exploiting them. This reaction shows also, however, a surprising ignorance on the part of some receiving governments and peoples of the true nature of Soviet aid in the context of Communist doctrine. If, occasionally, American aid has been unwisely, as I think, attached to political considerations, Soviet aid is determined almost entirely by such considerations, as Mr. Khrushchev has already boasted.

We have convincing, indeed conclusive, evidence of

the political character of Soviet trade and aid in the relation between the USSR and Tito's Yugoslavia. Here
there was no attempt to mask the political purposes of
economic relations. They were used brutally and cyni-
cally to bring pressure to bear on Tito, when he refused
to accept the dictates and the domination of Moscow.
This merely confirmed that foreign policy, in the case of
a state organized like Soviet Russia, determines trade.
In democracies it has often been the reverse.

The corollary of this is that trade with a Communist
state, while often to be encouraged for its own sake, is
not so likely to bring about an easing of tension as to
result from it.

This is something we should not forget in our political and economic relations with Communist governments. We should not try to confuse those relations,
and ourselves, by trying to apply to them our own ideas
and practices of competitive international trade. We
should also realize that these ideas, based on competition between traders and on the protection and advance-
ment of our own national trading interests in that
competition, often result in economic conflicts which
divide and weaken us politically. The Communist empire on the other hand is building up a closely controlled, self-sufficient group of states where trading arrangements within the group, and between it and other
states, are planned and organized in the interest of
Communist policy, particularly, indeed almost exclu-

sively, in the interest of Moscow. This development, parallel with what he considers to be a dissolving and inherently contradictory capitalist society, has undoubtedly encouraged Khrushchev to concentrate his attacks more and more on the economic sector of the cold-war front, as the most effective way of "burying us." If Western policy and diplomacy do not take account of this development and act vigorously and collectively to counter it, they will be foolish and shortsighted.

There are, unfortunately, few signs of the necessary cooperation and solidarity — and the strength that comes from them — on the Western economic front. Current European economic developments provide a good example of the difficulties in the way of securing it. We have here, in fact, a textbook illustration of the differences between the two systems: the Communist, with trade coordinated and controlled from one center for political purposes, and the democratic, where the relation between economics and politics is confused, but where the national interest, determined primarily by economic competative considerations, is usually paramount.

Six European countries have, after much travail and soul-searching, agreed on a Common Market. But the other eleven members of the Organization for European Economic Cooperation (OEEC) remain outside it. They wish to superimpose on the Common Market a broader but looser European Free Trade Area.

This would mitigate the effect of the Common Market arrangements on the trade of the eleven with the six, and yet retain for the larger group, more particularly for Great Britain, extra-European trading positions.

The six feel that their Common Market has an important a political as economic purpose — and they are right. They suspect that the eleven, particularly the British, wish to secure the economic advantages within the European groups without accepting any political commitments or without prejudicing special preferential arrangements such as those of Great Britain within the Commonwealth.

The two transatlantic NATO powers, the United States and Canada, seem to confine their interest to good advice, without even considering the possibility of converting the European into an Atlantic free trade area, whereas, in fact, they should be deeply and anxiously interested in this European development, for its success or its failure would be almost equally important for them. Failure would weaken and might destroy NATO. Success might split the Atlantic group economically between its European and North American members and encourage that continentalism, both economic and political, which is incompatible with the Atlantic idea.

Canada, with ties across the Atlantic and across the border, should be even more concerned with such a development than the United States, and anxious to do everything she can to avoid it. Continentalism has special implications for Canada which are as political as they are economic. After all, her seventeen million people share a continent and a manner of living with one hundred seventy-five million Americans.

This whole European economic movement shows the impossibility of separating economic and political considerations. It shows also how agonizing is the problem of trying to reconcile them within and between free states of a coalition in such a way as to give greater strength and unity.

There are further sources of strength, but I can mention only one which is the most important of all. It is the strength that comes from a freedom which is combined with discipline and responsibility. If we have this, there will be a power and steadiness behind our policy and diplomacy which no despotism can ever hope to achieve — providing, I repeat, because the proviso is all-important, that we use our freedom with wisdom and restraint, accept and discharge the obligations and duties that go with it. If we do not do this, then freedom, far from being a source of genuine strength, can degenerate into the weakness of anarchy and indulgence.

With freedom of the kind I have mentioned, there should go confidence in our own institutions, pride in our society, and determination to defend its values. We would be making a great mistake, however, if we assumed — as we too often do — that no such confidence and pride, with the strength that comes from it, can be felt by the citizens of a society founded on compulsion rather than consent. The Soviet Union has shown that it can.

Russian strength, I know, is based on a political and economic organization of society which subordinates every individual interest and aim to the requirements of state policy. This concept is opposed to everything that a free society stands for. It represents the negation of moral values and the destruction of human personality. Therefore it bears within itself the seeds of its own decay.

In the Soviet Union, however, it has created, at least for the time being, a pride and confidence among millions of people in many of the manifestations of its power. It has also produced a vigorous impulse for material progress and national development on the part of many people who feel that they are moving toward a goal which may seem to them better than any they have been able to reach in the past: the goal of a strong and prosperous, if socialist, society. They have been persuaded to accept, or compelled to accept, disciplines and privations unthinkable to us of the West, as the price of progress toward this goal. They are, in a political sense, a lean and hungry people, and they are driving or being driven along a route which is not as objectionable to them as it would be to us.

What do we oppose to this controlled, centralized, but surging society? Too often, merely the superficial clichés of the superiority of freedom and democracy and our way of life.

These things *are* superior to anything that Soviet Communism can produce, if we make them so in reality, not merely in words. The totally controlled and directed activity of a totalitarian state may confer some short-run advantage, in strength and organization, over our competitive and, at times, our complicating freedoms. But in the long run, there can be no salvation or no real security in any system in which a few despots, who have clawed their way to power and maintain their position by brute force, can enslave and debase the mind and soul of man.

While this "long run" is proceeding, however, we face our own difficulties and weaknesses. Are we sure, as we do so, that our social purposes in free democracy are steady and strong and healthy? There is good reason for anxiety. There are signs that those free institutions which should be the roots of our diplomatic and political strength may not be equal to the new challenges that face them. We should worry quite as much about this as about what is going on inside the Kremlin. It is not only Communism that is on trial.

We boast that there is nothing in Soviet Russia or Red China that can give the enduring strength that comes from a society of free men, refusing to be dictated to or pushed around, who are dedicated to a good purpose and willing to accept the discipline, sacrifice, and cooperative effort necessary to achieve it. But are our

Western democracies gaining that strength or losing it? We will certainly lose it if we permit our social and moral values to be degraded; if we make "bread and circuses" the aim of life and the policy of govern- ments; if worship of materialism makes us fat, and soft and smug.

The kind of freedom which brings these unhappy results will not impress the tough, implacable, and de- termined men who control the Communist world. I re- peat, therefore, if freedom is to be a source of strength, we who have it must show ourselves worthy of it, not by words alone, which can be easy and cheap, but by deeds: by putting first things first and by each accept- ing his full responsibility as a citizen.

I would say only this in conclusion. Even if we have the strength that comes from all the sources I have mentioned, the peace and security which are the goal of our policy and diplomacy will still be hard to achieve. It will require dedicated, persistent, and patient effort. There is no other way. There is no quick and easy solu- tion to the problems that divide and distract our world, our one and little world. The impatient assumption that there is, if only governments could find it, only weakens and confuses us. Equally unwise and unreal is the assumption that somehow we can find satisfac- tory solutions to world problems without the participa- tion of Russia or China, or both, in those solutions or in their acceptance.

The die is not yet cast for war. But neither is it cast

for peace. Events can still be controlled, trends directed, views altered. It is still possible to convince those we fear that they have nothing to hope for if they attack, and no cause for anxiety if they do not.

Neither power alone nor policy alone will save us. So what must we do to be saved?

We must have the right kind of power, moral, economic, social, and military, behind sound policy.

We must keep our domestic institutions — social, economic, and political — free, healthy, and progressive.

We must establish, accept, and maintain in our society moral values that will endure, that will deserve and receive respect.

We must keep our Western coalition firmly united for collective action in defense of these institutions and these values.

We must take full advantage of every opportunity, even more, create opportunities through a dynamic diplomacy, to negotiate differences with those whom we now fear.

In that course, followed steadily and not by spasms, with positive actions rather than panic reactions, based on a strength which is more than military, lies our best hope for a peace which will be worthy of the millions in our generation who have died for it.

THE FOUR FACES
OF PEACE

Nobel Peace Prize Lecture
Delivered at the University Aula,
Oslo, Norway, December 11, 1957

THE FOUR FACES OF PEACE

I cannot think of anything more difficult than to say something which would be worthy of this impressive, and, for me, memorable occasion, and of the ideals and purposes which inspired the Nobel Peace Award.

I would like, at the very beginning, to pay my tribute to the memory of a great man, Alfred Nobel, who made this award — and others — possible. Seldom in history has any man combined so well the qualities of idealism and realism as he did, those of the poet and the practical man of business.

We know all about his dynamite and his explosives and how he lamented the use to which they would be put. Yet ideas can also be explosive, and he had many that were good and were deeply concerned with peace and war. He liked to write and talk about the "rights of man and universal brotherhood," and no one worked harder or more unselfishly to realize those ideals, still so far away.

At this moment I am particularly conscious of the

wisdom of one of his observations, that "long speeches will not ensure peace."

May I also express my great pleasure at being again in Norway, a country to which my own is so closely bound by ties of friendship, freedom, and understanding. I have worked in a very close and cordial way with Norwegian representatives at many international meetings, and the pleasure I felt at this association was equaled only by the profit I always secured from it.

Perhaps I may be pardoned for putting any words I may have to say about peace within the framework of my own personal experience. During my lifetime greater and more spectacular progress has been made in the physical sciences than in many centuries that preceded it. As a result, the man who lived in 1507 would have felt more at home in 1907 than one who died fifty years ago if he came back to life today.

A great gulf, however, has been opened between man's material advance and his social and moral progress, a gulf in which he may one day be lost if it is not closed or narrowed. Man has conquered outer space. He has not conquered himself. If he had, we would not be worrying today as much as we are about the destructive possibilities of scientific achievements. In short, moral sense and physical power are out of proportion. This imbalance may well be the basic source of the conflicts of our time, of the dislocations of this "terrible twentieth century."

All of my adult life has been spent amidst these dislocations, in an atmosphere of international conflict,
of fear, and insecurity. As a soldier, I survived World
War I when most of my comrades did not. As a civilian
during the second war, I was exposed to danger in circumstances which removed any distinction between
the man in and the man out of uniform. And I have
lived since — as you have — in a period of cold war,
during which we have ensured, by our achievements
in the science and technology of destruction, that a
third act in this tragedy of war will result in the peace
of extinction. I have, therefore, had compelling reason,
and some opportunity, to think about peace, to ponder
over our failures since 1914 to establish it, and to shud-
der at the possible consequences if we continue to fail.

I remember particularly one poignant illustration of
the futility and tragedy of war. It was concerned, not
with the blood and sacrifice of battles from 1914–1918,
but with civilian destruction in London in 1941 during
its ordeal by bombing. It was a quiet Sunday morning
after a shattering night of fire and death. I was walking
past the smoking ruins of houses that had been bombed
and burned during the night. The day before, they had
been a neat row of humble, red brick, workmen's
dwellings. They were now rubble except for the front
wall of one building, which may have been some kind
of community club, and on which there was a plaque
that read, "Sacred to the memory of the men of Alice

Street who died for peace during the Great War, 1914–18." The children and grandchildren of those men of Alice Street had now in their turn been sacrificed in the Greater War, 1939–45. For Peace? There are times when it does not seem so.

True there has been more talk of peace since 1945 than, I should think, at any other time in history. At least we hear more and read more about it, because man's words, for good or ill, can now so easily reach the millions. Very often the words are good and even inspiring, the embodiment of our hopes and our prayers for peace. But while we all pray for peace we do not always, as free citizens, support the policies that make for peace, or reject those which do not. We want our own kind of peace, brought about in our own way.

The choice, however, is as clear now for nations as it was once for the individual: peace or extinction. The life of states cannot, any more than the life of individuals, be conditioned by the force and the will of a unit, however powerful, but by the consensus of a group, which must one day include all states. Today the predatory state, or the predatory group of states, with power of total destruction, is no more to be tolerated than the predatory individual.

Our problem, then, so easy to state, so hard to solve, is how to bring about a creative peace and a security which will have a strong foundation. There have been thousands of volumes written by the greatest thinkers of the ages on this subject, so you will not expect too much from me in a few sketchy and limited observations. I cannot, I fear, provide you, in the words of Alfred Nobel, with "some lofty thought to lift us to the spheres."

My aim this evening is a more modest one. I wish to look at the problem in four of its aspects — my "four faces of peace." There is Peace and Trade, Peace and Power, Peace and Policy, Peace and People.

PEACE AND TRADE

One face of peace is reflected in the prosperity of nations. This is a subject on which thought has changed greatly within the memories of most of us and is now, I submit, in process of rapid further change.

Not so long ago prominence was always given to economic factors as causes of war. That was at a time when people sought more assiduously than we now do for rational causation in human behavior. To the philosophers of the nineteenth century it seemed that there must be a motive of real self-interest, of personal gain, that led nations into conflict. To some extent there was. But in this century we have at least learned to understand more fully the complexity of motives that impel us both as individuals and as nations. We would be unwise to take any credit for that. The cynic might well remark that never has irrationality been so visible as in our times, and especially in relation to war.

We know now that in modern warfare, fought on any considerable scale, there can be no possible economic gain for any side. Win or lose, there is nothing but waste and destruction. Whatever it is that leads men to fight and suffer, to face mutilation and death, the motive is not now self-interest in any material sense.

If, however, we no longer stress so much economic factors as the direct cause of war, that does not lessen their importance in the maintenance of a creative and enduring peace. Men may not now go to war for trade, but lack of trade may help to breed the conditions in which men do go to war. The connection is not simple. Rich nations are not necessarily more peace-loving than poorer nations. You do not have to have poverty and economic instability, people do not have to be fearful about their crops or their jobs, in order to create the fears and frustrations and tensions through which wars are made. But poverty and distress — especially with the awakening of the submerged millions of Asia and Africa — make the risks of war greater.

It is already difficult to realize that a mere twenty years ago poverty was taken almost for granted over most of the earth's surface. There were always, of course, a few visionaries, but before 1939 there was little practical consideration given to the possibility of raising the living standards of Asia and Africa in the way that we now regard as indispensable. Perhaps only in North America every man feels entitled to a motor car, but in Asia hundreds of millions of people do now expect to eat and be free. They no longer will accept colonialism, destitution, and distress as preordained. That may be the most significant of all the revolutionary changes in the international social fabric of our times.

Until the last great war, a general expectation of material improvement was an idea peculiar to Western man. Now war and its aftermath have made economic and social progress a political imperative in every quarter of the globe. If we ignore this, there will be no peace. There has been a widening of horizons to which in the West we have been perhaps too insensitive. Yet it is as important as the extension of our vision into outer space.

Today continuing poverty and distress are a deeper and more important cause of international tensions, of the conditions that can produce war, than previously. On the other hand, if the new and constructive forces which are at work among areas and people stagnant and subdued only a few years ago can be directed along the channels of cooperation and peaceful progress, it should strengthen mankind's resistance to fear, to irrational impulse, to resentment, to war.

It is against this background that we should, I suggest, reassess our attitude to some ideas about which we have of late been too indifferent. It has been fashionable to look on many of our nineteenth-century economic thinkers as shallow materialists. We have, for instance, made light of the moral fervor and high political purpose that lay behind such an idea as free trade. Yet the ideals to which Richard Cobden gave the most articulate expression, at least in the English-speaking world, were not ideals about commerce alone. They visualized a free and friendly society of nations, for whom free trade was at once a result and a cause of good relations. It is a bitter commentary on our twentieth-century society that the very phrase "free trade" has come to have a hopelessly old-fashioned and unrealistic ring to it.

We all recognize that in the depressed and disturbed economic conditions between the wars an upsurge of economic nationalism was inevitable. But why should so many be so ready to go on thinking in the same terms when the conditions that produced them are now different?

We are too inclined to assume that man's today is more like his yesterday than like the day before yesterday. In some respects, I submit, the economics of our day are less different from those of nineteenth-century expansionism than they are from the later and abnormal period of depression and restrictionism that, just because it is nearer in time, still dominates much of our economic thinking.

The scientific and technological discoveries that have made war so infinitely more terrible for us are part of the same process that has knit us all so much more closely together. Our modern term for this is interdependence. In essence, it is exactly what the nineteenth-century economist talked about as the advantage of international specialization and the division of labor. The main difference is that excessive economic nationalism, erecting its reactionary barriers to the international division of labor, is far more anomalous and irrational now than it was when the enlightened minds of the nineteenth century preached against it and for a time succeeded in having practiced what they preached.

The higher the common man sets his economic goals, in this age of mass democracy, the more essential it is to political stability and peace that we trade as freely as possible together, that we reap those great benefits from the division of labor, with each man and each region doing what he and it can do with greatest relative efficiency, which were the economic basis of nineteenth-century thought and policy. In no country is this more clearly understood than in Norway, and in no country is the impulse to peace deeper or more widespread.

In this sphere, our postwar record is better than it is fashionable to recognize. Under the General Agreement on Tariffs and Trade there has been real progress in reducing trade barriers and in civilizing the commercial policies of national governments. The achieve-

ment so far has its limits, of course, and there have
been setbacks, but there has been more progress, and
over a wider area, than any of us would have dared to
predict with confidence twelve years ago.

Now the European nations are launching themselves,
through the Common Market and its associated free
trade area, on an adventure in the economic unification
of peoples that a few years ago would have seemed
completely visionary. Is it any more visionary to fore-
see a further extension of this cooperative economic
pattern? Is it not time to begin to think in terms of an
economic interdependence that would bridge the Atlantic, that would at least break down the barrier between dollar and non-dollar countries which, second
only to Iron Curtains, has hitherto most sharply di-
vided our postwar One World?

You will say that this is far too unrealistic. I can
only reply that in the past decade we have already seen
even more profound revolutions in men's political and
social attitudes. It would be especially tragic if the people who most cherish ideals of peace, who are most
anxious for political cooperation on a wider than national scale, made the mistake of underestimating the
pace of economic change in our modern world.

Just as we cannot in this day have a stable national
democracy without progress in living standards and a
sense that the community as a whole participates in
those standards, without too great extremes of wealth

and poverty, likewise we cannot have one world at peace without international social and economic progress in the same direction. We must have rising living standards in which all nations are participating to such a degree that existing inequalities in the international division of wealth are, at least, not increased. For substantial progress on those lines we need the degree of efficiency that comes only with the freest possible movement of commerce through the world, binding people together, providing the basis of international investment and expansion, and thereby, I hope, making for peace.

PEACE AND POWER

I now come to Peace and Power.

Every state has not only the right but the duty to make adequate provision for its own defense in the way it thinks best, providing it does not do so at the expense of any other state. Every state denies and rejects any suggestion that it acquires military power for any other purpose than defense. Indeed, in a period of world tension, fear, and insecurity, it is easy for any state to make such denial sound reasonable, even if the ultimate aims and policies of its leaders are other than pacific.

No state, furthermore, unless it has aggressive military designs such as those which consumed Nazi leaders in the thirties, is likely to divert to defense any more of its resources and wealth and energy than seems necessary. The economic burden of armaments is now almost overpowering, and where public opinion can bring itself effectively to bear on government, the pressure is nearly always for the greatest possible amount of butter and the smallest possible number of guns.

Nevertheless, defense by power as a first obligation on a state has to be considered in relation to other things than economics. For one thing — and this is certainly true of smaller countries — such power, unless it is combined with the defense forces of other friendly countries, is likely to be futile, both for protection and for prevention, or for deterrence, as we call it. This in its turn leads to coalitions and associations of states. These may be necessary in the world in which we live, but they do extend the area of a possible war in the hope that greater and united power will prevent any war. When they are purely defensive in character, such coalitions can make for peace by removing the temptation of easy victory. But they can never be more than a second-best substitute for the great coalition of the whole United Nations, established to preserve the peace, but now too often merely the battle-ground of the cold war.

Furthermore, the force which you and your allies collect for your own security can, in a bad international climate, increase, or seem to increase, someone else's insecurity. A vicious chain reaction begins. In the past, the end result has always been, not peace, but the explosion of war. Arms, produced by fear, out of international tension, have never maintained peace and security except for limited periods. I am not arguing against their short-run necessity. I am arguing against their long-run effectiveness. At best they give us a breathing space during which we can search for a better foundation for the kind of security which would itself bring about arms reduction.

These coalitions for collective defense are limited in area and exclusive in character. And they provoke counter-coalitions. Today, for instance, we have now reached the point where two — and only two — great agglomerations of power face each other in fear and hostility, and the world wonders what will happen.

If the United Nations were effective as a security agency — which it is not — these more limited arrangements would be unnecessary and, therefore, undesirable. But pending that day can we not put some force behind the United Nations which — under the authorization of the Assembly — might be useful at least for dealing with some small conflicts and preventing them from becoming great ones.

Certainly the idea of an international police force effective against a big disturber of the peace seems today unrealizable to the point of absurdity. We did, however, take at least a step in the direction of putting international force behind an international decision a year ago in the Suez crisis. The birth of this force was sudden and it was surgical. The arrangements for the reception of the infant were rudimentary, and the midwives — one of the most important of whom was Norway — had no precedents or experience to guide them. Nevertheless, UNEF, the first genuinely international police force of its kind, came into being and into action.

It was organized with great speed and efficiency even though its functions were limited and its authority unclear. And the credit for that must go first of all to the Secretary-General of the United Nations and his assistants. Composed of the men of nine United Nations countries from four continents, UNEF moved with high morale and higher purpose between national military forces in conflict. Under the peaceful blue emblem of the United Nations, it brought, and has maintained, at least relative quiet on an explosive border. It has supervised and secured a cease-fire.

I do not exaggerate the significance of what has been done. There is no peace in the area. There is no unanimity at the United Nations about the functions and future of this force. It would be futile in a quarrel between, or in opposition to, big powers. But it may have prevented a brush fire from becoming an all-consuming blaze at the Suez last year, and it could do so again in similar circumstances in the future.

We made at least a beginning then. If, on that foundation, we do not build something more permanent and stronger, we will once again have ignored realities, rejected opportunities, and betrayed our trust. Will we never learn?

Today less than ever can we defend ourselves by force, for there is no effective defense against the all-destroying effect of nuclear missile weapons. Indeed their very power has made their use intolerable, even unthinkable, because of the annihilative retaliation in kind that such use would invoke. So peace remains, as the phrase goes, balanced uneasily on terror, and the use of maximum force is frustrated by the certainty that it will be used in reply with a totally devastating effect. Peace, however, must surely be more than this trembling rejection of universal suicide.

The stark and inescapable fact is that today we cannot defend our society by war, since total war is total destruction, and if war is used as an instrument of policy, eventually we will have total war. Therefore, the best defense of peace is not power, but the removal of the causes of war, and international agreements which will put peace on a stronger foundation than the terror of destruction.

PEACE AND POLICY

The third face of peace, therefore, is policy and diplomacy. If we could, internationally, display on this front some of the imagination and initiative, determination and sacrifice, that we show in respect of defense planning and development, the outlook would be more hopeful than it is. The grim fact, however, is that we prepare for war like precocious giants and for peace like retarded pygmies.

Our policy and diplomacy — as the two sides in the cold war face each other — are becoming as rigid and defensive as the trench warfare of forty years ago, when two sides dug in, dug deeper, and lived in their ditches. Military moves that had been made previously had resulted in slaughter without gain, so for a time all movement was avoided. Occasionally there was almost a semblance of peace.

It is essential that we avoid this kind of dangerous stalemate in international policy today. The main responsibility for this purpose rests with the two great world powers, the United States and the USSR. No progress will be made if one side merely shouts "coexistence" — a sterile and negative concept — and "parleys at the summit," while the other replies "no appeasement," "no negotiation without proof of good faith."

What is needed is a new and vigorous determination to use every technique of discussion and negotiation that is available, or, more important, that can be made available, for the solution of the tangled, frightening problems that divide today, in fear and hostility, the two power-blocs and thereby endanger peace. We must keep on trying to solve problems, one by one, stage by stage, if not on the basis of confidence and cooperation, at least on that of mutual toleration and self-interest.

What I plead for is no spectacular meeting of a Big Two or a Big Three or a Big Four at the summit, where the footing is precarious and the winds blow hard, but for frank, serious, and complete exchanges of views — especially between Moscow and Washington — through diplomatic and political channels.

Essential to the success of any such exchanges is the recognition by the West that there are certain issues such as the unification of Germany and the stabilization of the Middle East which are not likely to be settled in any satisfactory way without the participation of the USSR. Where that country has a legitimate security interest in an area or a problem, that must be taken into account. It is also essential that the Soviet Union, in its turn, recognize the right of people to choose their own form of government without interference from outside forces or subversive domestic forces encouraged and assisted from outside.

A diplomatic approach of this kind involves, as I well know, baffling complexities, difficulties, and even risks. Nevertheless, the greater these are, the stronger should be the resolve and the effort, by both sides and in direct discussions, to identify and expose them as the first step in their possible removal. Perhaps a diplomatic effort of this kind would not succeed. I have no illusions about its complexity or even its risks. Speaking as a North American, I merely state that we should be sure that the responsibility for any such failure is not ours. The first failure would be to refuse to make the attempt.

The time has come for us to make a move, not only from strength, but from wisdom and from confidence in ourselves; to concentrate on the possibilities of agreement, rather than on the disagreements and failures, the evils and wrongs, of the past.

It would be folly to expect quick, easy, or total solutions. It would be folly also to expect hostility and fears suddenly to vanish. But it is equal or even greater folly to do nothing: to sit back, answer missile with missile, insult with insult, ban with ban. That would be the complete bankruptcy of policy and diplomacy, and it would not make for peace.

PEACE AND PEOPLE

In this final phase of the subject, I am not thinking of people in what ultimately will be their most important relation to peace, the fact that more than thirty millions of them are added to our crowded planet each year. Nor am I going to dwell at any length on the essential truth that peace, after all, is merely the aggregate of feelings and emotions in the hearts and minds of individual people.

Spinoza said that "Peace is the vigor born of the virtue of the soul." He meant, of course, creative peace, the sum of individual virtue and vigor. In the past, however, man has unhappily often expressed this peace in ways which were more vigorous than virtuous. It has too often been too easy for rulers and governments to incite men to war. Indeed, when people have been free to express their views, they have as often condemned their governments for being too peaceful as for being too belligerent.

This may perhaps have been due to the fact that in the past men were more attracted by the excitements of conflict and the rewards of expected victory than they were frightened by the possibility of injury, pain, and death. Furthermore, in earlier days, the drama of war was the more compelling and colorful because it seemed to have a romantic separation from the drabness of ordinary life. Many men have seemed to like war — each time — before it began.

As a Canadian psychiatrist, Dr. G. H. Stevenson, put it once: "People are so easily led into quarrelsome attitudes by some national leaders. A fight of any kind has a hypotic influence on most men. We men like war. We like the excitement of it, its thrill and glamor, its freedom from restraint. We like its opportunities for socially approved violence. We like its economic security and its relief from the monotony of civilian toil. We like its reward for bravery, its opportunities for travel, its companionship of men in a man's world, its intoxicating novelty. And we like taking chances with death. This psychological weakness is a constant menace to peaceful behavior. We need to be protected against this weakness, and against the leaders who capitalize on this weakness."

Perhaps this has all changed now. Surely the glamor has gone out of war. The thin but heroic red line of the nineteenth century is now the production line. The warrior is the man with a test tube or the one who pushes the nuclear button. This should have a salutary effect on man's emotions. A realization of the consequences that must follow if and when he does push the button should have a salutary effect also on his reason.

Peace and People has another meaning. How can there be peace without people understanding each other, and how can this be, if they don't know each other? How can there be cooperative coexistence, which is the only kind that means anything, if men are cut off from each other, if they are not allowed to learn more about each other? So let's throw aside the curtains against contacts and communication.

I realize that contact can mean friction as well as friendship, that ignorance can be benevolent and isolation pacific. But I can find nothing to say for keeping one people malevolently misinformed about others. More contact and freer communication can help to correct this situation. To encourage it — or at least to permit it — is an acid test for the sincerity of protestations for better relations between peoples.

I believe myself that the Russian people — to cite one example — wish for peace. I believe also that many of them think that Americans are threatening them with war, that they are in danger of attack. So might I, if I had as little chance to get objective and balanced information about what is going on in the United States. Similarly, our Western fears of the Soviet Union have been partly based on a lack of understanding or of information about the people of that country.

Misunderstanding of this kind arising from ignorance breeds fear, and fear remains the greatest enemy of peace.

A common fear, however, which usually means a common foe, is also, regrettably, the strongest force bringing people together, but in opposition to something or someone. Perhaps there is a hopeful possibility here in the conquest of outer space. Interplanetary activity may give us planetary peace. Once we discover Martian space ships hovering over earth's air-space, we will all come together. "How dare they threaten us like this," we shall shout, as one, at a really United Nations!

At the moment, however, I am more conscious of the unhappy fact that people are more apt to be united for war than for peace, in fear than in hope. Where that unity is based on popular will, it means that war is total in far more than a military sense. The nation at war now means literally all the people at war, and it can add new difficulties to the making or even the maintenance of peace.

When everybody is directly involved in war it is harder to make a peace which does not bear the seeds of future wars. It was easier, for instance, to make peace with France under a Napoleon who had been kept apart in the minds of his foes from the mass of Frenchmen, than with a Germany under Hitler, when every citizen was felt to be an enemy in the popular passions of the time.

May I express one final thought. There can be no enduring and creative peace if people are unfree. The instinct for personal and national freedom cannot be destroyed, and the attempt to do so by totalitarian and despotic government will ultimately make not only for internal trouble but for international conflict. Authority under law must, I know, be respected as the foundation of society and as the protection of peace. The extension of state power, however, into every phase of man's life and thought is the abuse of authority, the destroyer of freedom, and the enemy of real peace.

In the end, the whole problem always returns to people; yes, to one person and his own individual response to the challenges that confront him.

In his response to the situations he has to meet as a person, the individual accepts the fact that his own single will cannot prevail against that of his group, or his society. If he tries to make it prevail against the general will he will be in trouble. So he compromises and agrees and tolerates. As a result, men normally live together in their own national society without war or chaos. So it must be one day in international society. If there is to be peace, there must be compromise, tolerance, agreement.

We are so far from that ideal that it is easy to give way to despair and defeatism. But there is no cause for such a course or for the opposite one that leads to rash and ill-judged action.

May I quote a very great American, Judge Learned Hand, on this point: "Most of the issues that mankind sets out to settle, it never does settle. They are not solved because they are incapable of solution, properly speaking, being concerned with incommensurables. At any rate . . . the opposing parties seldom do agree upon a solution; and the dispute fades into the past unsolved, though perhaps it may be renewed as history and fought over again. It disappears because it is replaced by some compromise that, although not wholly acceptable to either side, offers a tolerable substitute for victory. He would find the substitute needs an endowment as rich as possible in experience, an experience which makes the heart generous and provides his mind with an understanding of the hearts of others." *

Above all, we must find out why men with generous and understanding hearts, and peaceful instincts in

* New York: Alfred A. Knopf, 1952.

their normal individual behavior, can become fighting and even savage national animals under the incitements of collective emotion.

That is the core of our problem: why men fight who aren't necessarily fighting men. It was posed for me in a new and dramatic way one Christmas Eve in London during World War II. The air raid sirens had given their grim and accustomed warning. Almost before the last dismal moan had ended, the anti-aircraft guns began to crash. In between their bursts I could hear the deeper, more menacing sound of bombs. It wasn't much of a raid, really, but one or two of the bombs seemed to fall too close to my room. I was reading in bed, and to drown out or at least to take my mind off the bombs, I reached out and turned on the radio. I was fumbling aimlessly with the dial when the room was flooded with the beauty and peace of Christmas carol music. Glorious waves of it wiped out the sound of war and conjured up visions of happier peace-time Christmases. Then the announcer spoke — in German. For it was a German station and they were Germans who were singing those carols. Nazi bombs screaming through the air with their message of war and death; German music drifting through the air with its message of peace and salvation. When we resolve the paradox of those two sounds from a single national source, we will, at last, be in a good position to understand and solve the problem of peace and war.